The Apple-Broadcast

By Peter Redgrove

The Collector and Other Poems
Routledge & Kegan Paul

The Nature of Cold Weather and Other Poems
Routledge & Kegan Paul

At The White Monument and Other Poems
Routledge & Kegan Paul

The Force and Other Poems
Routledge & Kegan Paul

Work in Progress (Poems 1969)

The Hermaphrodite Album (with Penelope Shuttle)

Dr Faust's Sea-Spiral Spirit and Other Poems
Routledge & Kegan Paul

In the Country of the Skin
Routledge & Kegan Paul

The Terrors of Dr Treviles: A Romance
(with Penelope Shuttle)
Routledge & Kegan Paul

Sons of My Skin: Redgrove's Selected Poems 1954-74
Routledge & Kegan Paul

The Glass Cottage: A Nautical Romance
(with Penelope Shuttle)
Routledge & Kegan Paul

From Every Chink of the Ark and Other New Poems
Routledge & Kegan Paul

The Wise Wound (with Penelope Shuttle)

The God of Glass: A Morality
Routledge & Kegan Paul

The Weddings at Nether Powers and Other New Poems
Routledge & Kegan Paul

*The Sleep of the Great Hypnotist: The Life and Death
and Life After Death of a Modern Magician*
Routledge & Kegan Paul

The Beekeepers: A Novel
Routledge & Kegan Paul

The Apple-Broadcast
and other new poems

Peter Redgrove

ROUTLEDGE & KEGAN PAUL
London, Boston and Henley

First published in 1981
by Routledge & Kegan Paul Ltd
39 Store Street, London WC1E 7DD,
9 Park Street, Boston, Mass. 02108, USA and
Broadway House, Newtown Road,
Henley-on-Thames, Oxon RG9 1EN

Set in IBM 11 on 12 Baskerville by
Columns, Reading, and
printed in Great Britain by
St Edmundsbury Press, Bury St Edmunds, Suffolk

Library of Congress Cataloging in Publication Data

Redgrove, Peter.
    The apple-broadcast, and other new poems.
    I. Title.

PR6035.E267A87 1981 821'.914   81-10587
ISBN 0-7100-0884-8   AACR2

ISBN 0-7100-0985-2 (cassette)

Contents

Poems marked with an asterisk have been recorded on a C90 tape by the author.

Preface

Grateful acknowledgments are due to the following maga-
zines and anthologies in which certain of the poems first
appeared: *Akros*; *Ambit*; *Bananas*; *Decadal: Ten Years of
Sceptre Press*; *Delta*; *Encounter*; *A Garland of Poems for
Leonard Clark*; *Helix*; *Hibernia*; *The London Magazine*;
New Statesman; *Pacific Quarterly*; *Perquod*; *Poetry Book
Society Christmas Supplement 1980*; *Poetry Now(BBC)*;
Poetry Review; *Samphire*; *Sceptre Press Pamphlets*; *South
East Arts Review*; *Temenos*; *The Times Literary Supplement*.

Particular thanks are due to the Editors of the *Poetry Review*
and *Helix* for their special supplements.

I have read twenty-two of these poems on a C90 tape available from the publishers.

Dedicated to the memory of G.M.

A wineglass overflowing with thunderwater
Stands out on the drumming steel table

Among the outcries of the downpour
Feathering chairs and rethundering on the awnings.

How the pellets of water shooting miles
Fly into the glass of swirl, and slop

Over the table's scales of rust
Shining like chained sores,

Because the rain eats everything except the glass
Of spinning water that is clear down here

But purple with rumbling depths above, and this cloud
Is transferring its might into a glass

In which thunder and lightning come to rest,
The cloud crushed into a glass.

Suddenly I dart out into the patio,
Snatch the bright glass up and drain it,

Bang it back down on the thundery steel table for a refill.

SPRING

Even the bicycle-oil smelt of daffodils.
The full round drops slid into the little orifices.
I made my chain glitter.

1

I pumped the pedals with my hands, the bike
Inverted on its handle-bars and saddle,
And made the wheels shine like mirrors,

And they whirled like skirling puddles;
My pleasure was intense to think
Of the scented oil spun into the machine's recesses.

She came out into the sunshine from the house;
She wore a kind of bloomers and a blouse.
She mounted on her wheels like summer cobwebs.

The air was scented with my father's daffodils.
My pleasure was intense to see her cycle
And to watch the air puffing through her blouse,

Past every recess in her perfumed fields.
I opened my collar to the breastbone
Like a proper cyclist, and my erection

Was angular and pleasant on
My pointed pommel as I pedalled after
Along sweet-smelling roads, the scented oil

Spinning through my glitter.

CORNISHMAN VISITING

He sponges the salt off his hat
Preparing for his London visit.
The yachts glide outside his window

Like ladies in long dresses, like
Walking trees blown along by their blossom.
There was light over the horizon, as though

His car were nearing the old cathedral town,
But it was the Moon rising.
He rubs affectionately the old leather hat,

Round is like the Moon, and salt
Betokeneth the moony sea;
He kneads the darkening dubbin deep; he

Will polish his hat till
Windows appear in it, until it flames
Upon his head like the whole sun

Caught in a round window. His good shoes:
They are clotted with mud and cracked.
They shall stay that way. Why should anybody

Consider feet beneath that resplendent head,
Or, if they drop their gaze, he does not dissemble,
Sloshing through native soil even in golden London's streets.

THE BRITISH MUSEUM SMILE*   *Tape A 1' 03"*

None of the visitors from teeming London streets
Smiles. The deeply-lined downtrodden faces
Elbow the galleries. The sphinxes inside smile
And the colossal faces.
The face of a king with shattered legs
Smiles. And the guards smile. Their solitude
Forms into a smile and the patience
Of all the seated faces in navy uniforms
On the little chairs with the deeply-marked cushions
Smiles. They have caught it from the sphinxes
And the colossal kings and the powerful scribes
With the stone incense-bowls who smile sweetly
Over the smoky crowds. Some of the smiles
Are printed on the air from the faces of the guards,
And the stone faces have dissolved a little in the air;

3

Passing through and through the smiling galleries
Rubs inch by inch the face into a smile,
The smile of the king you pass (whose legs are sand),
The imagined absent smiles of the drenched nereids
Whose headless robes blow back against their flesh
In many folded smiles, whose smiling heads
Are museum air; the mummies
With their gasping toothy grins
Under the polite smile-paintings of their coffin-shells
Lumbered here by ship and block and tackle
Scattering a trail of smiles; elsewhere
The nereid heads are pebbles or sand,
And who picks up the pebble smiles at its smoothness;
(And the sleek sand is made of microscopic nereid heads
Turning and kissing in the water of the tide
The smiles rubbing from quartz lip to lip,
Dissolving in the sea and flying on spume;
The mariners inhale, and smile.)

Such smiles have flittered down
Like pipistrelles of Egypt on to the faces of the guards
And the smiling guards know something unknown to their
    crowds,
Something fallen from the sphinx that patters down
To fit you as you sit still on a stool
Polishing with your back those polished stones
For twenty years, or among those polished volumes
Not reading, but learning that smile. It took
Four thousand years to teach that smile
That flutters in these galleries among the guards
Who exchange mirrored smiles across glass cases; how
Did stone first catch it, that virus smile?

The spider creaking in its rain-coloured harness
Sparking like a firework. In the cold wind
Round the sharp corner of the house,

In the cold snap of that wind,
Many turned to ice:
Circular icicles.

My father lifted one off
Very carefully over the flat of his glove.
When I see these hedgerow webs

It is always with the sighing of the sea
In my heart's ear; it was at the seaside
In the smell of sand and tar that I first

Understood the universal perfection
Of these carnivorous little crystals
Coiling from their centres like the shells.

They were cruel and beautiful
At the same time; abominable
And delightful; why else did the silly

Flies dart into them to be drunk
Up like horny flasks, as if
The pints of beer had veiny wings —

If I could see those dartboard webs
Surely they could. They are doorways
To death and the mandala-sign

Of renewed and centred life. And this one,
Here, look, with its array of full lenses
(For the thread is fine enough for minutest

5

Beads to catch and roll the light in strings)
Is like a Washington of the astronomers,
Planned, powerful, radial city, excited by flying things,

At every intersection and along each boulevard
Crowded with lenses gazing upwards, pointing light.

THE KINDERBRUNNEN

The Kinderbrunnen, the popular cool fountain-garden,
This is where the white stork left them,
This is where the parents found and brought them home.

And they may return and play here
But not play too late:
The black stork flying through the dark could take them.

I see lost children dancing in the dusk
Like small fountains strayed from their source,
Little white flames of water keeping their shape

Of skipping children and dancing babbling children,
Or standing still in the dark, disconsolate children.
I come closer, and there are only fountains.

The stork has taken them back,
Or the darkness has turned them all to water.

THE LITTLE HORSE

Moonprints struck in sand, the horseprints
Circling the glossy beach; the little horse
Full of power that must be used
Galloping, galloping; the tan raincoat
Of the girl rider, her thick
Brown stick lathering the pale flank,

Who canters round and round the wet sand
Each hoofprint flowering swiftly;
In the wind, dark flanks, light manes blowing:
The sea made of horses;

A dashing squall of rain, the white hooves
Of water galloping down the valley stones;

Now the wind prefigures there
All blowing locks, all manes;
Did the sea make horse and rider?

Who hammered the bridal bridles and caught like a surfer
Under a lathering saddle the wave of horse-blood and bone?

Was it the wind galloping out of the woods, through the
     waves,
Like a little horse shattering the thin salt pools,

Was it done among these dense valley
Hemlocks quivering like hoofprints of sea foam?

WILL

I catch my father's damp last breath
In my flared praying nostrils.
The steel hulls in the dock

Are ringing like great bells to their repairs,
Notes that shake the floor, beyond hearing.
He has gone to his nether world, the place appointed,

Or his breath has gone there, to the world of rushes,
The wind's furrowing roads, the ghostly thoroughfares.
Above the sheepfields and the dying-room

Supersonic flight rams the air
That has passed the lips of all,
This breath the latest,

As to the booming hulls the grey sea cleaves
Snorting with salt nostrils the breath of all.
My father's damp breath brushes my cheek again,

The clouds are full of bosomy weeping mothers;
The damp breath from the stony beaches reaches past me,
Outside the window the grass is furrowed through with it,

With gasp of death nourishing the living.

LIGHT*   *Tape A 6' 08"*

Every seed a recording of light
That flashes in days and nights;
The feathery plant-seed

Like a travelling candle-flame;
The melon full
Of patriarchs of light

In yellow halls
Bearded in succulence;
(The secret that accompanies a man

8

Synopados, yet he
Is a shadow to that light);
People lit inside, like houses

In the darkness, waking houses;
There were sieges of
Nocturnal emissions;

Could they have borne them, they would
Have known that the forgotten encounters
Took place in a light that trembled

To the lightest touch, breath,
Like a candle-flame or a travelling seed;
The beehive, the candles

Rolled of light consumed in the old coal forests;
The sun, who giveth light of his own body;
The bees that issue

Out of the copper-coloured sycamore that drinks
Up light out of the vessel which is
Its own multitudinous shadow;

The storm that blankets the land
Out of the thermal corridor of the sun —
The electric lights fail, in the sound

Of thunder we light candles. Our seeds
Record the candlelight, which is
Romantic. Leonardo was right:

There is a direct and minute channel
Thin as a hair between eyes and gonads
Through which the light passes; they ripen

In the thunderstorm, in the candlelight, and
Particularly when the clouds explode earthwards in wet
    flames.

PAGAN POEM

It soars, the stone house,
The cottage of Selene,
Over the beach of scuttling stones.

The sea's steel waves are magnetised,
The beach knocks head against stone head
Drowsily, is hypnotised, click-clock,

Nodding up at the singular head on high.
Magnetism pours through the highly-polished air.
Meteors are fine flints falling

Like those rolling beach-pebbles
Struck into fire by silver-plated air.
When many fall in swarms we say

It is the dress of Isis,
Her dress of stone and light all pleated.

WHIRLING MEDALS

I went into the cinema, where the screen
Flickered with preserved fire that was dead,
It was when I emerged that I saw the living fires,

The sun shorn of its many beards,
The rim red and clear, quietly sinking.
There is a fire everywhere that is preserved by what it burns.

The elm-buds are like red beetles which are also flames of the
    tree,
They flame amazement and open in strict harmony;
There is the magnolia's white bush-fire, like a shower

Of fangs; and in the shop by the bush
I have seen the watchmaker enter to his bench
Littered with broken dials and cogs

To screw them into intact timepieces, meshing
Chiming webs that shake with the seconds
And as he shrugs his jacket off and speaks

I glimpse the gold fire of his teeth;
And there is the micro-second beat
Of the clear flicker of a bee's wings;

And the sun's rim clear and red, sinking,
And against the disc a warship smoothly glides
Bristling with pointers like a malicious clock

Intact, but put together wrong, with muzzles
Of canned fire and whirling medal engines.

THE CLAY TIP

The cone drilled out of its own brink
Of smoking powder,
Solid light in a heap:
The floodlight on the clay-tip.

Its own grasses bind it,
Its briars and bushes,
The talc ghost
In its flowering sheets,

Pyramid-spirit with wrapped paws,
Spook of the cups and saucers,
The glazed brambles and roses
That having endured the furnaces

Are raised to soft lips
Millionfold at four o'clock
In all the porcelain cities,

Ramshackle ghost of all the fine vessels
Towering in its country,
Raked with chinasmoke winds
That cast dazzling shadows,
Heap of uncreated crockery:

Water deep in its pit
Catches the full moon
White as a tip, flood-lit;
I stare at the white moon
And watch red poppies flower over its tall small sister.

CLOUD-RUSTLING

He seeds the rain-clouds with silver-salts,
His little silvery aeroplane like flying Jesus,
He steals my rain that should have fallen on my hills,
It is cloud-rustling;
He milks them all over his meadows.

Who owns the 2,000 million tons of water
Floating heavy as cathedrals in the skies of America?
Jesus does, in his aeroplane.

The rain begins.
I zip up my fly and open my collar.

The ocean asleep and restlessly dreaming,
Thick-grassed with my rain, ancient pampas,
The clouds that belong to me
Escaping over the spacious earth,

The sun a great broad soldier
Muffled in his grey trench coat —
Let him come out!
In gold beard and gold helmet, a Kaiser!
Tearing through the rainbow flimsies,
Throwing down gold sandals for all the waves!

DELIVERY-HYMN*   *Tape A 8' 15"*
(During birth the baby's head rotates against the *os crucis* at the back
of the mother's pelvis.)

See! the Woman is coming,
A Christ child in sun's rays
Painted across her clothing.

The Ancient of Days is in His heaven,
Dangling like a parachutist in angelic cords
Among white wings feathering and beating;

The Ancient's finger is hushing His nose,
He is white-nightied in womb-clothes,
Curled currents of birth-water are His beard;

His Mother's true presence rustles through all her veins,
He knows the whole Torah,
His skull bowed and in the mouth the small thumb,

Preaching the thumb-suck sutra from the hollow womb.
See, under her bellyskin little knuckles punch up at heaven!
The Mother croons over her cathedral-dome

Hymns to her Ancient who will emerge into light and form
Fragrance and other wonders in His good time,
But is first to be crucified headlong on bone.

Now He is full-bearded and in the nave,
His serene locks are curled pulsations of the water,
He is warm-shirted in membrane,
And knows the whole Torah.

(The Woman is coming now, and some Christ spills
Bright-red over her clothing.)

IN THE GLASS HOUSE

Glass-shrimps lighted up like ghosts
Pedalling through a wavery weedy landscape
A glass bicycle which is oneself,
Adjusting one's fishing-rod arms,
One's toolchest face;
Showing all one's guts in ghostly armour
Like the transparent dead of Holy Land;

And to enter a rocky underwater harbour
Where a lobster once again casts rigging
Like a full ship making empty ones
Among a landscape of harbour crabs like lichened cisterns
Or boulders with eyes and doors and munching casements;

In the spinning convent
Of water that is life that has taken its clothes off;

In the lofty one's low house —
Fishhouse the water-goddess —

Where watersnails keep the aquarium fronts clean
Like travelling padlocks off the lips of drowned men.

A PAPER HOME

A paper home for burning at the graveside;
In the pouring rain the ghost-house would not ignite,
As though the ghost struggled,
It fluttered in the wind between the tombs.
I snatched it up and tore it across;
God tore the sky with thunder,
A brilliant door swung open, slammed.
The mourners were content;
The sky ripped for their friend
Lacking the grey wings of smoke to take him up,
The snapping beak of fire.

AT THE STREET PARTY*   *Tape A 10' 15"*
(*Jubilee 1977*)

Water makes her way, accustomed
Into all places, through mire as an eel,
Through the air as a hawk,

She gets past the obliterator of forms
Because she is the transformer,
Gets past clothed in food-chains,

Buckled into such sappy, stretchy satchels,
As wasps and gnats, such expanding
Revelation luggage as you. And the air

Which separates forms: to breathe with joy
Through the double nostrils, the nosethrills,
And to smell at the street-long table

Of the jubilee party in the open air
The head of my son as a mark of tenderness,
Smelling my sweet son in salutation,

15

Like fresh-baked bread mixed with the smell of tar
Of useful rope, sitting at his banquet
Under the street lamps with the other youngsons,

And — I could live on the smells of it —
He is warm and slightly sweating,
My sweet son, having drunk wine,

And I can smell the wine escaping from his hide,
And on the table the scones brick-brown
And the fruits arranged in castles,

And water making her way into our forms with joy
By way of wine and beer in cool pewter
As we drink to each other, and the pewter has its scent

Its faint eternal scent of tin, and the crowned
Heads above smiling wide on the flags, bending and rippling
Taking into wide mouths their great draughts of air.

THE MOISTURE-NUMBER

The moisture-number of the species:
Humans are two-thirds clear water;
It is the cloudiness that speaks,
The stagnant turbid water that fights and talks
Under the flooding clouds, on the torrential battlefields
By the hurtling river that bleeds.
The peeled fish swarm and couple
In the pond of skin, the water-bag
Between the bones.
Water departs like a soul,
Like a white shadow,
Leaving a little dried crust
Between bones like a cleated footprint:
Travels over the world, water
Enters fresh wombs of brackish water.

THE NUMINA AT THE STREET PARTIES* *Tape A 12' 19"*
(Jubilee 1977)

That river-stone, in its glistening shirt of water;
The ghost paths of the marram as it rustles papyrus
Over dry dunes; you hear the tinkle

Of the glass grains embedded in the hairy whisper.
The numina
Show through here and there.

A mirror nailed to a tree, reflecting the waterfall,
It guides the car as it reverses
From the driveway, but it hangs the fall too

In the tree, gushing like a fountain,
Inexhaustible balsam. Just so the street
Is strung across with flags rippling above us

As though our tables were laid beneath
The surface of a broad river; the kegs
Are trestled and tapped and flowing amber, the many

Tablecloths joined end to end and held by big ragged
Pieces of paving on the street-long tables,
The lemonade like jugged sunlight, the brown scones

Castled in lopsided towers. Then the breeze drops
And the flags are lank, the street party falls silent
And nobody smiles, except the crowned pictures

Which smile on everybody and into which
The numina have withdrawn. Then the breeze rustles
And the street streams again like the river-rushes:

It was for a moment as though air stopped in astonishment,
And parted to stare into those crowned
And tuppence-coloured faces, then flowed on.

The power and safety of those faces will enter
Our beds and help us make young persons like them
Brown as scones, and safe. Its mirror-shirt

Slowly dissolves the river-rock, the marram parts
For ghosts to glide away over the dunes
Darkened with their momentary dew, spirits

Shredded by the violin grass; the numina move on.
An old woman taps for attention on the glass
And bends her ear to the Queen's lips for an answer;

The numina clamber high to thunder, come back in shining
    rain,
The air is full of white kings muttering, crowned
With flashing lights. We have feasted

Beneath the lake, now wrestle under the streaming rain
With blowing tablecloths like the drenched shirts of rivers.

GWENNAP CROSS*   *Tape A 15' 13"*

Suddenly, it is autumn,
The convolvulus chars
With a fleshy scent,

The little Saxon Christ
Stands among his ebbing flowers.
He is carved from oolite

With his arms outstretched,
He stands in his stone loop
Supported by a thick shaft.

The prehistoric seas strive
And the result is this same Christ
Speeding through the corridors of time

18

With arms outstretched and welcoming
As though the shaft into the ground
Were those self-same corridors of stone time,

For the sea has set as stone, and we,
We carve it into welcoming gestures.
And since the light that fell into the great tree's head

Became that plant, and the beasts
Nibbled and their bones were inundated
And sacrificed to geology, therefore

Is it any wonder that this stone
Became our patron?
Do you see a person here,

Or just a stone?
Do you see a person in the moonlight,
Or is the Moon just a round stone

With a hare carved on it
Flying without a shaft? If
It is just a stone, why

Does it fly, spreading
Magnetism like feathering wings
Whose beat you see reflected in the tides

Whose claws pluck at the water-margins?
I pause, and look up at the full disc.
Someone has carved a man there

Sitting safely in a boat
On its floodlit surface.
I kiss the head of the Gwennap Cross,

It is a hard and odorous stone
And tingling, but the smell in it
Is as though I kiss

The head of my baby with its rinsed mossy smell.

SALUTING WILLA

(The great boulder at the mouth of Boscastle harbour in N. Cornwall
is sometimes known as 'Willa'.)

The warship glides in like a malicious buffet of cutlery.
Willa's petticoats are slamming under her stone dress
Like iron doors detonating deep within the rock,

Shuddering through the feet that tread her slate sills,
Her blow-hole smoking and saluting
That has buffed for centuries her inside corridors

With the sea's rifling from which they shine like glass
As for military inspection. The warship's personnel
Line their greymetal platforms at attention,

Salute with ship's guns the rock that has been firing
Its cannon at high tide longer than artillery
Was ever thought of, or steel could float,

The hollow rock volleying from its caves
Returning thunder with thunder
Back to the buoyant anvil hammering

Among the windcells and the catspaws tautly anchored.

THE DEAD AND THEIR CHILDREN*　　*Tape A 17' 33"*

The river in our country, it bears slopes
Of transparent mud,
It polishes and polishes, squandering,

This white river, whose glass shoulders
Spring transparent wheat, and bread
You can see through, which is

Perfectly wholesome for the dead to eat, and doing so
We grow see-through, and in due course
Invisible, when we are known as

The truly-dead. Then we do not need
Bread any more, not even ghost-bread;
The habit of eating dies hard.

You may come out
Into the street and see us laying
Our table of dust, polishing and polishing

Until every grain is fit to eat off. Meanwhile, elsewhere,
Wax gathers slowly in the humming cave,
Dark wax, glistening with honey,

Polished and polished again
By the bees' jaws among the polish
And glitter of their wings, ready to be spread

On bread, thick slabs of bread, thick brown
Opaque bread and honey for the mortal children.

THE SIRE OF BRANCHES AND AIR*   *Tape A 19' 04"*

I

The sire of branches and air.
The low waters begin
To give off their cunny smell;
It means rain is near.

We have the emergency edifice,
The umbrella, which is a cross
Between a city suit and an office.
The moist wind bends the trees

Which have acquired presence
And their extra dimension
From this alluring smell
Forced through their budding branches

From hammered reservoirs like cold pewter shields
To which they add their own pinch of cunning.
They are threads of pulse
To which the breeze

Puts its own beating fingers
Gently, like a bearded physician.

II

The branches toss with such question,
And swell with such abandon,
I think each tree is a child at play,

It has donned the wind
Like a playsuit that thinks up games,
And falls thoughtfully into its quiet folds,

Then the resumed wind mounts
The stiff sire of branches,
It is a ghost trying on bodies,

22

Cassette

A C60 cassette of Peter Redgrove reading
21 of the poems in *The Apple Broadcast* is
available to order from any bookseller
(ISBN 0 7100 0985 2) price £5·15 + VAT (in 1982)
or in case of difficulty from the publisher.

The price may be increased in later years
without notice.

For your convenience an order form
is attached.

Please supply one cassette of
Peter Redgrove *The Apple Broadcast*
ISBN 0 7100 0985 2

Please send me an invoice.
I enclose open cheque.

☐☐☐☐☐☐☐☐☐☐☐☐☐☐☐☐☐☐ Credit card
(delete as necessary)

Name ....

Address ....

....

....

Order to your bookseller or to . . .

ROUTLEDGE & KEGAN PAUL
PARTRIDGE HOUSE
NEWTOWN ROAD
HENLEY-ON-THAMES
OXON RG9 1EN
ENGLAND

Streaming over the land and letting them drop
After their battles.
A great face opens laughing

In that tree-head, and in that other
Head, the hair smarms flat as a seal.

I think that elsewhere this spectre also
Is a child; that somewhere in a nursery
Just over the treetops, a child's

Sleeping body lies in its white bed,
Emptied of the small omnipotent ghost
That can overturn a countryside

Of leafy timbered rooms, like a burglar
Passing invisibly through green walls;
Now large pawmarks appear printed

Across the leafhead and satisfied
The spirit of the child condenses
From the muscles of wind,

Lays itself along the little body and
Shrugs its way back into the angelic countenance.
I open the nursery door on my way to bed,

There is a knowledgeable smell of rain;
I shut the window and notice how still
The cunning trees are on the ridge after the storm.

EARTH SHAKES AWAY ITS DEAD LIKE *Tape A 21' 50"*
CRUMBS FROM A CLOTH*

They have smoothed their mounds down,
The dead, they have healed the soil and gone;
All is smooth lawn, a trifle long.

Where there was once an orchard of stone,
They have left, however it was done,
Only a seeding lawn, a trifle long

That works in the wind like television:
Across grass pictures, viewless sprinters run,
The prints of an invisible force flying,

Every wing-beat distinct in the grain
Of winnowing stalk and shadowing stem.
They have picked up their skeletons,

The people of clay, they have walked in their bones,
Plucked up their gravestones and not scythed the lawns;
I cannot tell how it was done;

All vanished into grass, a little long.
They have pulled up their static stones,
Their texts, and tucked them under their arms,

They have gone off like borrowers in the evening,
In the twilight returning dull thick tomes;
I wish I knew how it was done,

The graven texts gone.
All that is left is a shivering lawn;
Under it I can't tell where who was lain,

Or whether or how he is coming again,
The writing gone. Shadows hunt on the wind,
Calf-deep in cool grass I could hardly be stung

By these shadows of snakes, by these skimming scenes
Healed into a park; my feet laved in soft grasses
I wade through green streams.

Where are they hiding? I want to meet them
Now, before they are departed and quite gone.
Will they not be clean

And cool, like this wind-driven lawn,
And like the wind flying into the unknown,
Not by still text kept down, or solemn stone?

THE PRIMER

The Primer is sorrowless.
Patsy and John are always fine.
The Postman marches up the gravel path briskly.
He carries a party invitation. He is on time.

It is always fine in the Primer.
Patsy and John are sorrowless.
Breezes pull no mouths down in the tall elm trees,
Nor are these willows weepers.

Nanny wears her proud uniform that is without smut,
Rustling blue and white like the summer air;
Under sheer smile and sleeveless shirt still
John's crotch is as uncomplicated as his Teddy Bear.

The Primer is a lie, in which only truth is told:
Bad boys in poor houses tell fibs and not John;
Patsy blubbers sometimes, just like a girl.
Mother is utterly sterling. Daddy never comes home.

It is always sunshine in the Primer,
Mother, Nanny, Patsy and John are sorrowless;
Daddy wrote the book, then closed it and will not return
Though paper eyes keep watch for him, fresh and furrowless.

ONE OF THE PLANET PEOPLE AT STONEHENGE

It was blood and I mistook it for tears snuffling.
Look, Flossie, is this not a marvellous thing!
I blow a hankie moth-shape from a bloody nose.
White breath beats from my lungs in wing-shapes,
Or in mothy whispers feathers from my lips.
What a place this is, what a holy wing-palace!

And will the white angels advance through these portals
Dragging their plumage like parachutes
Through the trilithons? Ah, suddenly
The light is in my ring:

It is picking up the stone broadcasts before moonrise,
The premier Stone, docking on Stonehenge — or, as I like
To say, Stonehinge, the door between the two worlds.
Those wings were wings of ghosts pulling their shadows after,
Shadows of blood, I mean, ebbing across this flat stone,
For the Moon, like any other ship, is visited
By fluttering moths like souls, who are
Themselves the shivery reflections of a greater soul
Whose shadows are what we call solids: look at all the lovers
Gliding between the stones, their hands
Moth-walking over the stones. The night-jar calls,

The voice of night straining on its hinges,
And the Moon rises, casting
A tremendous round weir of light,
As we were promised, combing us of our shadows.
Do you not feel cleansed, like angels? Drat!
This nosebleed prints hankie-shadows of them and of
Some outrage half-credited between my own stone portals.

THE MIDAS VARIATION*   *Tape A 24' 20"*
(*For R.G.*)

He broke down some dividing wall
In his flesh and changed to Midas. The solitaire
Shining on his finger had become opaque

Faceted gold. He embraced
His companion of the work and she became
Gold, cold and pure, her clothes

A miraculous tissue of only the one colour,
And her skin continuous with it,
Welded to her clothes. He felt ill

And hurried to the toilet. He watched
Between his legs into the pan
Expecting that the faeces would be pure gold

But they were faeces. He bent
And prodded them with that finger, the ancient
Steaming coils became soft pure gold.

The pleasure of this erected his penis,
He touched it: it became a staff of gold.
Now he had a crock of gold, and a gold staff

And a gold friend: what more could he desire?
He placed the magic finger with its solitaire
On the kitchen chopping-block (which stained

Into gold) and meat-cleaver swinging
Severed it with a thunk. The block
Was grainy gold, the disappearing finger rolled

On the stone-flagged floor which flooded
Sunny, into gold. He looked
At the severed member's surface, it was closed

27

With a diaphragm of gold round which
Drops of ordinary blood oozed.
Back in the lab just off the kitchen

He found his golden sister of the work
Moving about the room quickly, tidying up,
Laughing between gold teeth at the sheer pleasure

Of being gold. 'I wish,' he said,
'I had touched my own head and become like you';
'But I would have stayed immobile if you had not cut

Off and sacrificed that gold-contagious finger.'
'Still, we've got plenty to live on,' pointing to the floor,
'Yes, and you've got a penis suitable for gold girls.'

'I wish my brain were gold like yours'; 'When I whisper
Thoughts to you, your brain glows gold
Like coals in the fire; do not ask

To be dead,' said the golden shade.

ROCK, EGG, CHURCH, TRUMPET

There is a churchy rock
Mothy with seagulls
Looking as it would fly

If only they would beat together
Their bread-mould pinions,
Fly like an angel of rock

With a stubble of wings;
Ripples pass over the rock
As though it were planted thick

With wheat that is mouldering.
The gulls mew-mew.
The rock that has indeed become a church

Is crazy with its wounds,
Having been sliced from the hill and
Blown up from it, and fitted together

On the same hill, a little higher:
The windows moan, the hinges shriek,
It is carved into weeping angels, it is

Thickly-set with their wings and open-mouthed guttering,
And is something between an egg and the rock;
Church is one of three kinds of feathered stone

That cannot fly. An egg is full of feathers,
A sealed stone globe, the pebble of a bird
That has roosted and will roost on a grey rock

That ripples its hide with feathers and shadows
In the creaming tide; and the church
Bellows with song attempting to take off

With the hymning engine of pewed people
Throbbing to us across the waves.
Stone is not just such an inertia —

Look at the little gymnast
Swinging to music along parallel bars
On those long bones; listen to the Tibetan

Flute of bone and the shoulder-blade violin
Strung with gut, and the creamy violin
Held high in the claws of a feathered angel;

The stone moon carved with a hare
Swoops over the feathering sea
That beats like the one tidal wing of the world —

Pull the cold bone up to your lips, Trumpeter,
Bark out with your angel-breath laden with spirits!

THE TURNING STARS

Orion hammering up there like brass studs
Nailed into the black wood of the vault,
Great mask above the trees of African fogwood

Declaring with its brass fixings
That the God floats above us
Riveted to his vault;

We sneak cowering past the tree-trunks,
For the star of honey and wine is a rivet
And the stud of influence that causes 'flu,

We should not let its light glide into an open pupil.
Any of these stars could switch our luck,
Twitch life out of our hands.

How deep the well of the eye is in the daytime,
You can see your stars in it,
There is an erotic and ghostly atmosphere

Which tells me my star is changing;
Which side is showing now? The trees
Become like dark stars with outstretched beams;

Look! the very trees have lost their substance,
They are thin stockings of sheer silk
Smoothed over their lasts of timber:

That is all a tree is, yet how much!
Cellulose, and rustling leaves, and living silk.
The dusk is falling, like gentle silk

With its breezes; Orion rises,
The ghostly air is erotic again with wet
Like star-drifts through the trees,

Earth's swivelling beaded mists
Made entirely of lenses
Nailing watchful studs to the hairy leaf,

Hammering out the constellation Web.

THE CAVE

He stands under a bright sky
With a rotten apple in his hand. It
Is a winged apple, for it is full

Of codling moths, and down the blackened
And webbed paths the seed still hangs
With its leafy corridors, its heaps

Of autumn fruit. The wings of the moth beating
Stir the leaves in the seed; the apple-egg
In his hand is struggling to hatch.

Every wing-beat is a new thought, then the thoughts
Speed from his hand and the sky is dark
With fringed wings and heavy apples, and the wings

Dip and he hears the deep breathing
Of the dead. After this, the conjurer in the head
Can develop his act. In it the clothes

Of the audience shall come to life, and strip
Themselves off the sitters, prance and dance
In the aisles, and the conjurer shall stand aside

And the clothes shall waft on to the stage
And clothes will pull chains of clothes out of hats,
Clothes will saw other clothes in half.

The naked audience, feeling their power
Stripped from them, their talking clothes, their
Eloquent masks and attitudes, shall sit

Attentive, naked as pips, while
The handless, headless, hollow clothes
Shall pull themselves through each others' textures,

And pray with hollow sleeves held up, and sacrifice
By unbuttoning and falling off the air, and fly
Like moths and lie in heaps like leaves,

The conjurer thinks of his act, holding the winged fruit
In which the seeds sit watching the moths eat.

FIELD THEORY

The stars that stand for pardon and love
Shuddering in the sky like silent gongs;
And God's boaters, his water-boatmen,

His clouds and their spinning shadows,
His white headless hats standing tall,
Even His stains are shining-white and walk

Scrabbling over us on their airy water-legs.
The vast slow weather-whirlpool turns
And rustles like a young woman's rainy clothes.

There is a great white ear floating high up there,
Listening; then the white hunter comes
Sliding with his buckler through the night:

Orion. Morning: the daisy-lawn
Photographs the sun in holograms
With its yellow core and white influence

Stretching over the sky, and the green stem
Swivelling. The newspaper arrives, pulpy columns
Of dead and wounded marching with charcoal banners.

The deerpark is by the sea, the ocean asleep,
Restlessly dreaming; the strenuous sparrows
Sketch out a whirling liverish face high in the sky,

A mile-long apparition made of feathers.
Thus the day passes, mixing its weathers,
Compounded of weathers. If the Moon

Is just a stone, how can it fly?
This evening wine, with the Moon
Buttoned into it, can't be bad

For me, can it, it smells so spiritual, and
The black shadows that are gathering are secondary
Shadows merely; the primary ones are cast

Off by the sun in its whirling and are rocks
And trees, the earth itself,
A hologram of the great sun, a signature it wrote.

THE EGGS

The bird with bone on the outside,
The smooth egg. Melt butter over your egg, let
The yolk shine in its clouds!

Once she poured clarified melted butter
On herself, so that she might shine
Like the moon, and remarked how she could turn

Round and round inside her buttered skin, and if
You take a handful of wet clay and press
A pip into it it becomes grapefruit,

But only if the seed awakes to your touch,
Only if you shine to the seed.
The morning after,

Her shine seemed gone, rainbowed off
In crowds of bathroom suds, relaxed
Over the warm and scented waterskin, but at breakfast

She smiled again like last night and the shine returned
To everything. She spread butter
Over her soldiers and dipped the strips

Of toast into hot egg, the shine
Broke out of that sealed egg, I swear it,
Like a radium of the kitchen (I saw

Our child shine before she was born:
In my dream I rubbed the best butter
Over the pregnant dome and as though

It were white paper windowing with the grease
The first thing that I saw was the smile
Of the babe looking out at me,

Her sucking thumb, and then how she
High up in the clear butter of her mother floated).

THE VERY RICH*   *Tape A 27' 05"*

The more secret angel, the bird
Inside the gold bar; the ingot rings
As you strike it with the little hammer,

34

And the ringing turns to birdsong; the very rich
Can always hear birdsong. I was surprised
To feel how soft the gold was, I could

Dent it with my fingernail, I could have carried
The value of a fiver away
Under my claws, it is as soft

As blackboard-chalk, you might write across the stone walls
Of the vaults with the ingot, or scrawl
Accounts there. When they closed

The safe door that looks like a battleship's
Immense gun-port, all wheels and bolts
To contain the gold explosion, the valuta

Solid as dynamite with light and force
And his cheque-book the fuse, I was surprised again
That the gold did not continue shining in the dark,

But it was ordinary dark lightless as graves.
This was when I struck a match and hit the bar
And the singing began. Having seen

So much gold, it has never stopped for me. It corrupts,
Yet it is incorruptible; it is like
The sunlight of earth that is free to all,

Yet it is beautiful and locked away. I think
Of the bullion-van on its way to the lock-up
Missing its way and smashing into the stone

Castellated Mint wall. It leaves
A big streak or splash of gold where it impacts
After the car of men has burned away,

Gold rammed into the stone singing with the collision
And sooty with the human grease, but I polish
And polish it clear and see the whole world

In a mirror of gold set in corrupt old castle stone.

THE EYE OF DR HORUS*   *Tape A 29' 16"*

They have the medicine-eye of brass.
It is the brass qualification of the Doctor,
He who holds the Eye, his shingle;

It means that the Man in the Eye
Shall never die, a tall story:
That is to say, the expression in the eye

Which is the man will never die. I have seen
The family face in the stately home
Conducting us between the family portraits,

Introducing himself as 'guide', the never-dying.
I have seen my expression in the eye
Of my great-aunt in bombazine

Watching from her sable photograph;
I caught it quizzing me from my contemporary self
When I cracked my head slipping on the soap,

Seeing her emerge from the black stars that swarmed
Through the bathroom mirror, my concussion-portrait
In shocked white on white walls. I see it lurking in a glance

From under the baby-fat, and as the months go by
I see the soft milk-mask melt off,
And one is looking at me steadily

With myself hanging like a picture in her eye's centre,
The eye's apple. *I am imagined.*
And in the hooded eyes of the doctors

And nurses crowding round my sickbed
Will I be imagined well, or will I know
From their emptying gallery of eyes that they are losing

Their grasp of my expression and it is time to die?
Oh, Doctor, polish the brass eye and make it eternal
So that your patients and yourself may live

Long lives in the countenance of your art,
The magical glance of one who will not lie to you,
While the family face is lounging

On every stoop along the dusty streets.
Yet in the baby's eye I see myself supplanted,
I can see that I am passing through

And withering as her gaze grows; yet she is me,
And that man in her eye will look out of her sons at her,
The baby-fat melting away and the gaze steadying.

In Egypt and in our land, the eye and the seed,
The eye and the potato-shoot equally
Bear the same name, from which the next life peers.

PERSIAN FEAST

The nodding Persians sleep.
It is an emaciating and a diuretic wine. Cupbearers
Slip fine wine over the lips of sleepers.

The wine-bibber relaxed as a corpse is like
His own footprint in clay
Moistened with crushed grape,

Grapes trodden in the clay, with some flowers,
The clay blissfully dreaming in its imprint
Like a solid shadow of himself,

The shadow his dream cast
He who has gathered himself up and gone on.
The muttering Persians nod,

The fine wines glide over sleepers' lips
Under the stars like little boxes of bright ointments,
The Sprawlers' Banquet,

Every head glorious with its grease,
Shining, laved with honey,
All the dark skins deepened with this massage,

Precious oils spent on the head
Running down into the beard of the sleeper,
And this perfume is his very name

While the King anointed in God's name nods on his throne.
The sleepers are noiseless as oil,
Oil that is without noise and is improved by pounding,

That is a wanderer and embracer of surfaces,
And a rainbow, as the dream is,
And as God's words are which were made flesh

And poured forth upon us all like ointment.
A veiled and dainty sober old matron smiling
In charge of the categories of ointment

Watches the grease melting from their locks
Which shines them graciously in firelight,
Her people glowing like bearded stars with ointment

Over whose sleeping lips the fine wine slips.

STREETS OF THE SPIRITS

The trees the streets of the spirits
Speaking in whispers with the green lips,

Those who trot invisibly down the long alleys
On air-horses that bound

From tree-crowned hill to copse,
Printing hoofmarks that heal again;

The reeds the carpeting of the spirits
Through which their immense feet swish

On their way to walking over the lake
Down the sliding street of the river to the ghost-maned sea;

Puddles, the exquisite mirrors of the spirits,
The thin plates of rain

For the invisible faces that bend down
And press the whorls and loops

Of their rough visage against the responsive waters.
Or do trees hustle spirits on their way

Swat them around the globe,
Propel them on their adventures

By beating, the reeds by rustling,
The mirrors by showing the way back into the sky?

I think of the air like an immense cope
Of silky glass stirred by the valiant trees,

Like welded ghost, or a bell ringing
That rumples and unrumples with its notes,

The spirits the music of the trees
Beating like the clappers of a world-bell,

By a command of their deeply-interlinked roots
With their chases beating world-music into everything.

LE CABARET BLANC

There is preaching among the little buttery flowers,
And behind the whitewash pellicle, fossil-packed masonry,
In the nightclub there is a sequin-covered dancer

Like the mechanism of a watch that has got free
To prance and glitter in the spotlights,
The liberated ghost of a watchmaker

Made of movement and innumerable diamond cogs,
Twitching like a rachet from the hips:
Years at the floodlit bench have made of him light and pace.

Now, outside, gazing through the quickset stars
Thorn-bunched in the smokeless air
Is like looking through God's watch,

Through all the wheels with diamond teeth; and I pray
That the hour will not be long striking when the chime
Shall echo round the cabaret's washed walls, and God

Wake up in everybody's glass. The clouds
Go to bed secretly, turning over and over,
Tucking in at the horizon, and unveil

That satin drenched with wheels again. There are tombs
Pierced with long grass as though their doors
Were shot through with radiant flights of arrows, and the
    moon

Is rising on the draughty lake, where silver
Sequins grind and bump in long streams noiselessly.

THE OCCULTIST

I

The Son of Man, etc.
The Son of Man hath nowhere but dew.
Isis is called Dew, in her flasks —

Suddenly laying down a silver sheen,
Mirror of dew of a million lenses,
(All-dew assembled in the sky below)

And the moon caught in it, gliding through it,
Travelling with a soft thunder
Like a landscape in the sky,

Like the scape of a cliff with the sea thundering within it,
Clouded, as the sea hangs clothes up in the rugged chalk
    wardrobes,
With the oceans thundering softly across its ragged face.

The Son of Man drinks only the dew, etc.
The Seven Women seek one husband through the dew and
    stars,
The dew around them and the dew within,

The dew that is virgin fire at the centre of them
Where the four elements are projected ceaselessly in
    movement,
The sea, that is taken apart and put together again,

The grey sheet that is whisked off the meadows
And put together again
In the web, or in the greying raincloud

That shoots into the web again, to hang;
The stone above, that great finale of the system,
The stone gliding through the water that is drink,

Wherein the Son of Man lays his face and laves it, in the
    dawn.

II

Next, there is a substance that shines like a fish's eye,
And is left behind by the desiccation of the sea;
Perhaps it is the firestone from which the spark springs,

The silex packed with closed eyes: hit it,
And the eyes spring forth.
He dips into the fiery soul of the egg his buttered soldiers.

The searchlights cross the field that very night,
And their beams converge in every dewflask hanging,
The first laboratory of the Son of Man.

Like the occultist, dew and fire have no fixed abode.
Only their abodes, candle,
Flint or grass are what manifest the powers

That have nowhere to lay their heads for long, like dew.

THE UNCRUCIFIED

The yew-walk is as long as the church,
The branches seem as thickly-pleached
As the church-stones are set

But there are innumerable shaded doors
Hidden in the perspective
Of the black vaulting

From where I am standing
At the head of the dwindling
Lanceolate corridor

In the hush of sooty pillars
Watching the few needles of light slide in.
Then suddenly a bird darts from one side

And across as though there were no
Building of trees there at all;
And another, and then again, three;

This nave is scampering on all sides
With birds, the fat air-mice, buttery
With the little bits of sun, and

This fastness is transparent
Perfectly to birds, and to bird-song,
I realise I had not heard the birds singing

Until I understood they visited the yew-walk
So freely, flying. Now along the gravel path
I crunch between the tombs that are fast-closed.

By the South door stands a cross of stone
In which is carved a small man
With outstretched arms who is not

Crucified, though they say he is.
Once I saw this shape, the tall
Stone pillar with the bulbous end

And the happy man concentrated at the tip
As the gladness of the phallus
Welcoming, now I see

It is like a corridor to fly down
And he is shown to me
As though flying through the stone. I recall

They say how dreams are always accompanied
By sexual excitement: how could it be otherwise
As the winged caress of vision

Flies through flesh and bones, singing.
The small man stands
At the tip or threshold, crossing

Through, not crucified as we were told.

NEXT DOOR ON THE LEFT

The people in the next cottage who have
Moods black as thunder, I hear them crying out,
I hear them banging their saucepans, they put out
Marrowbones and raw meat for the bluetits,
And the birds come thick as flies to eat flesh.

The people in the next cottage whose table-salt
Is a sea-salt echoing from the thunderous waves,
Whose flies crawl like birds or small thunder over the meat,
The black skulls polished with the whitechina streaks:
What kind of person are they to teach

Songbirds meateating? They cast a black rock
Into the torrent and it sprays out in white bloom,
Their faucets knock like Krakatoa, I see them
In the garden watching the sunset-wrack

Arm-in-arm where their sheets have dried all day
Crackling like whips in the strong wind,
And at night they bed in sheets vibrant
With light and air, and through the wall
I hear their copulation thundering and pelting,

And in the dawn marrowbones greasy with dew
And bluetits hovering with beakfuls of meat
And a new day; such neighbours
Are training piranha-birds who would strip me as I stood

Weeping to a skeleton, then beak the teetering bones
To weld their strong eggshells
And turn me inside-out, the egg-meat
Of my flesh sealed tight in bone-shell,

Having to crack my own bones to achieve birth,
The human cuckoo, my little movements of death
Feathering to chick-plumes in the jostling nest;
By these neighbours — who are they? — parcelled up,
Reversed, redistributed, posted, flying the nest.

FULL MEASURES

I

People sailing down the river
In wooden vessels between the magnificent trees,

Leafy cisterns of river standing in their own shadow
Like avenues of barrels in cool cellars

That grope up to feel green in the skies,
River flowing upwards from miraculous bottles

Of willow contentedly rowing the river to God;
The true source hovering, blinding white, over the mountains;

And it is moving with a note, like great brown lorries
Of goods trains rumbling full of water, though it is

Like one long umber room of sequent chambers
Sliding through each other, which are pulses

Echoed from the rainy source, the rocks
It bounds down, the turfs that hold, one long room

Broadening and full of sunlit motes
And recapitulating ripples. Quantities have paused

To fill the trees, to construct shady paths
Before they volplane back to water in the flat

Veined drops of autumn. Other water
Pauses in its stages like passengers

Passing in wooden vessels between magnificent trees.
The sky's bartender in blackening whitecoat

Prepares his biggest drops, full measures.

II

On the boat made out of trees I drink my beer
And hold it up to pledge the river; it matches,

It is mainly water, and stays a while in me
Rejoicing and transmitting visions

Of where it's been, some of which I see. The ocean
Drinks at the river's mouth, the sky

Bends down to sup the waves, and water
Runs invisibly up the wind-ladder

Disclosing as it flies great ice-ships,
Snow-rigged, spunglass frigates, until it is too heavy,

Can go no further, and returns barking,
A great hound of thunder. And on the evening river

Under the leaves the water flies
In winged drops with a sticker drinking

Freely from all a special heavy beer
Fermented in our veins for generations

Travelling in our veins like walking rivers.

FROM THE LIFE OF A DOWSER

Water is bad for him, much too exciting.
He runs away to Cornwall and drinks
From the sparkling well, *Fenten ow Clyttra.*

As he lifts the tin cup he wonders,
Trembling like the water in the cup,
What it will show this time, after so long,

They have boiled his water, made him drink tea,
That is stunned water, but he believes it thinks
As it tumbles over rock, breaking white,

Or streams into the high air, breaking white,
Or lies below its lintels in old stone wells
Pondering like some long transparent god

Waiting to be consumed and joined to more of him.
The Dowser believes, looking into his cup
Where air-bubbles in the water cluster

On sheer mirrors like silver tods of grape
And feels like that god about to drink
Some vineyard that is moonlit. He shuts his eyes,

The water is cool, and tin-tasting,
A spectre of earthy darkness brushes by
His throat, and disappears. There is nothing more.

He gets up from his knees and brushes them, regards
The avenue of long grass in which he stands

That burrows into the hillside with at its end
The stone lintel to water like an open wardrobe
With clothes of light flung about the grass

The dew-sheen and the spidery coronets
Which shiver like those bubbles of the well,
And a triple stone head on the cross-beam leering.

Still nothing more. Maybe this
Is enough to dig a well into the hill for,
To sculpt it and process, to make pilgrimage,

But then, why here, when everywhere
I break some slate in a damp cutting and water springs,
Whenever I dig my garden down into the water-table,

Prod five finger-freshets in the ferny turf.
Water is everywhere, and I think with it,
And remember with it, inside this rock

(And raps his knuckle on his brow),
And speak with it, as the clouds make scenes
And scrolling pictures, like a god

Opening his mouth and bellowing through
Lips and beards of water, water streaming
Through him like a fall or force, when

The frowning clouds in white coats came for him
Like falls walking and he forgave them. Now water
Is still in him, and well, and pondering.

MIRIAM*   *Tape A 31' 16"*

Blood becoming wheat as it flows,
Somehow; the smiling bull
Watching over its shoulder at me

48

Over the sheaf of wheat
That springs from its cut throat
Like golden veins harvested.
Then the Princess: her twelve
Companions merely the mirrored
Reflections of one Princess
Who has a candle
That never goes out,
Moreover, once it shines on a place
That place is full of candlelight
And dancing shadows of twelve companions.
Bull, and blood that is food,
And Princess who is a drop of the sea,
'Miriam' as she is called,
A candle everlasting as the sun —

I have seen too much, says the Soldier,
To be married to the Ropemaker's Daughter,
To wear her necktie or dance at that wedding!
(A disguise of the Princess his wife, no less.)

GRIMMANDERSON ON TRESCO

A pocket Moonbible by the lacy shore,
A Ladybible of God the Mother,
Of ultimogeniture: the lad
Freshest from the womb inherits
Nothing but fortune's favour
And extraordinary companions
On the electrifying adventure.
These are not wrinkled scriptures
In fly-dirt size on india paper
Crisp as a fly's wing; it is
A story-teller's stout handbook
Of basic situations: the old king
Needs a wife, the great toad like a wasted moon
Waxes Queen aboveground; the battered soldier

Steals a tinderbox, and has
Dogs with piercing sight at command;
A white snake tasted from a covered dish
Imparts to the breakfasting king bird-speech.
You do not cling to the scripture,
You improvise with spirit.

On a rock above the delta where I read it,
A fruitfly shares my apple with me,
Tastes my fingers and walks about my palm
With its bicycle-pump tongue.
It has a horny frame
Dwindling delicate as a tropical shell;
It is the self-same shell-stuff
As those beautiful thin million ears
Listening inside the Atlantic fetch.
It has cobbled spectacles it cannot take off.
On this dry day my friend
The painted conch with wings,
Sips, sips at my sweat-beads,
As thirsty I puncture my apple's skin,
Drink its fountains of juice stored up for me,
Read Grimm's bible by the spumy shore
Where fruitfly swaggering like an inheritor sups
Sweat-apples of my palm's seamed thoroughfare.

USING THE DARK

'Ripe winds bring supple peachwood pens;
I shall whittle me a set to last all winter,
Writing of the light with white peachwood.
There are not many powers, there are fewer than we think:
There is the power of white and the black power,
And grey may be a power, vibrant grey, but I'm not sure:
The Cabbalists call grey the left side of the Face,
The Inner Robe of Glory and the phallus,
The standing stone and the straight line, the tower,

The Vision of God face to Face, the Second Glory,
But I think of the moon, mediating the dark, and I'm not
    sure . . .'
'You're stocking up with fine images for grey winter,
Reading Dion Fortune in the pub,
Filling yourself with glitter like an Xmas tree,
The eleven coloured sources of God, Kether the Crown,
Chockmah, Binah, Chesed, Geburah,
Tiphareth, Netzach, Hod, Yesod and Malcuth,
And mysterious Daath, the hidden Sephirah:
The tree of life, glitter of power, cascade
Of God brought by collision at the tip
Of black with white, and these the hovering sparks.'
'Think of the sceptre and the crown
Studded with diamonds dug by starving Africans,
As eyes of the black dead brought back to witness . . .'
'The diamond dead eyes open Parliament brilliantly, African
    ghosts
Process through the greystone halls . . .'
'Yes! let's make it black and white on Saturday night,
The opulent cream skirt of the good Guinness sweeping
Down the vaulted gullet like a black lady in a white nightie
Gliding towards her marriage with my flesh . . .'
'Not Jewish, surely, Irish,
And very ancient.'
                    'Ironish, actually,
There's a brewery at Helston, and the black Cornish slugs,
Heavy sliding ingots, glitter up its yards
In the moonlight that is grey witness to the white dew
Declaring like diamonds . . .'
                    'And the black power
Of the good Guinness with the white talking head.'
'And all winter white peachwood pens
Dug into the black ink for testimonies,
Down the page the poet's ink
Sparking brighter than all the Christmas-trees!'
'What a programme! Will the dead come back, do you think,
Their coffins on the tree like Christmas parcels,
Will you unwrap these presents from the dark?
Will they walk with white feet across your pages,

51

Whispering invisible between the lines,
Can you see ghosts by the Christmas-tree lights,
Or is everything transfigured, knowing its source?
Or will you light your way with Guinness
As now, drunken monarch opening piss-Parliament?'
'Being drunk is like being dead, flashes of light,
And waves in the head, these spirits in the mouth
Come from the death of grains, who shall say
That the small death does not bring a candle to the gulf?'
'I thought light in a child's eye was the purpose of the tree.'
'Then we are the dead, haunting the rich child's house.'

RENFIELD BEFORE HIS MASTER*   *Tape B 0' 00"*
(Renfield was the lunatic in Dr Seward's asylum who assisted Count
Dracula during his English expedition, and who loved to eat flies.)

I

He was eight when he started earning
His living in a silk factory;
The big bales, corded with twist,

The incipient peignoirs, the feminine slink.
Was he a spider at all, once?
The managing director nipped the nub

Of his silk-web, at his shiny long table
Sipping at telephones, and his workers, caught,
Buzzing and gossiping

At the endless benches of their lives along which
The silk slid in thin rivers.

II

He liked bouncing in the bales, sneezing into
Their dusty canvas hides like crabby shells —
Lying outstretched over them

Gripping the cordage with one's hands
And one's feet braced, one's loins
Buried in some special penknifed silken gash, and one was

That male spider with a bellyful of silk oneself.
He would watch the canteen flies,
All possible silk, and at home

He kept in a pearly bottle choked with gossamer
A lustrous great spider he fly-fed; he had become
Clever enough to snatch them on the wing

Wondering at how the beautiful webs
Could yet be spun out of the corrupt glues
That were the fly's food; he mused upon

Those husks caught up in orrery rounds,
Emptied of all purpose, yet white
And winged as angels. He knew

The silk of his employment was spun by worms
Of a moth, and dreamed of feeding that moth
To his spider, the silk would be redistilled, radiant

With the light and pulsing beauty of all the trembling moths
That spin silk clothes for the babies of themselves
Wrapped and cross-clawed like an Egyptian Karast.

III

The butterfly or the sulphur-moth sucking at her weed
Is only one of the beauties; her transformation
To thin taut threads under the same sun on which the spider

Dances to eat her is another of them,
The skeletal patterns of cracked shadows in the sun;
And the beauty of the crabby lichen-back

That chucks her loins from side to side
Like Lola Montez, and tiptoes out
To wrap on tautened lines her prey in bales,

Is yet another, as he thinks
Drowsily of sleep, that great spider
Bending down to suck his soul from his face,

Kissing face to face, and turning it
Into that sensitive web which fills the nightworld
And catches fluttering dreams for nourishment;

So Renfield's madness or peculiarity
That loved the creatures so
The rest of us despise, led him

Fearlessly into the night of dreams,
Young silk-factor, where he met the master, Vlad,
Who fed him endlessly from thin soft hands.

IV

Who fed him endless streams of drops on wings
Like mother's milk, choice flies, and told him:
'Be that spider whom you fear, I, Vlad Dracula,

Will so transform you, as you wish,' and showed him how
Life flows in liquid drops, through fangs,
Creature to creature, in chains of drops like webs,

And whose work he did, so long as he was strong,
Guiding the young white girls to dance
Upon the webs without being caught by Death,

Raising them to drink as It did, spiderly,
Until fly-swatting Van Helsing clapped his fat palms
Smack and said 'No more of those,' wiping hands

Stained from the stake down immaculate spun hose.

ORCHARD WITH WASPS

The rouged fruits in
The orchard by the waterfall, the bronzed fruits,

The brassy flush on the apples.
He gripped the fruit

And it buzzed like a gong stilled with his fingers
And a wasp flew out with its note

From the gong of sugar and scented rain
All the gongs shining like big rain under the trees

Within the sound of the little waterfall
Like a gash in the apple-flesh of time

Streaming with its juices and bruised.
Such a wasp, so full of sugar

Flew out within the sound
Of the apple-scented waterfall,

Such a gondola of yellow rooms
Striped with black rooms

Fuelled with syrups hovering
At the point of crystal,

Applegenius, loverwasp, scimitar
Of scented air and sugar-energy

Shining up his lamp-tree tall and devious
Given utterly to its transformations

From sharp-scented flowers to honey-gongs,
Giver and taker of pollination-favours,

A small price for such syrups and plunderings,
Its barky flesh, its beckoning fruit,

Its deep odour of cider and withering grasses,
Its brassy bottles and its Aladdin gold-black drunks.

BEES AND MOSS

I look down a well
Deep and dark as a swaying poplar,
At the bottom a disc

Flashing white as if the moon indeed
Were caught in the plunging tree's tip,
And at the side of it a little notch

That waves and then calls out
In booming organ-echoes,
And that is myself, the reflector.

They say you can see stars
In the daytime in a well,
The stars ministering to the dead

In the underworld with their milk rilling
From bright glasses. I want
To clamber down and discover

The secret rooms built in the shaft-side
And what's in them, even if
The only treasure is secrecy, or the iridescent dead

Nourished on starlight. Perhaps
I could live there and learn to be
A minor official of the volcanoes

Commissioned to ignite the well
As one of the preliminary acts
Of the great 'quake,

Water blown like a fizzing shell of glass
Thousands of feet high to smash
On the blue heights and put the sun out,

Or a fountain-master whose task it is
To adjust the faults and flows,
To tug the strata straight or tap them

So that the lowly well at the hill-foot
Is first a spring overflowing a parapet
Then a fountain arching in beautiful bows

Bestowing moss from spray on all the boulders
Where bees to quench their thirst swarm close as moss.

VISIBILITY NIL

A salt-cured house deep in the dunes.
A telephone box half-full of sand,
Full of sunlight netted

Like a mayfly's wing, and the sea prowls
As I dial my number. My smile
As I talk to the outer world

Is well-hung, but quite provisional.
I used to meet with her at night
In the scented garden for the blind,

By the staring pattern carved upon the stone.
The blind were quite invisible at night,
As dunes are, shifting in their slippers.

My contractor prevaricates and loses time,
The sand-hills go on revising their horizon,
Erasing big stones with their little rocks;

I need to plant trees, they will supplement
The wicker windbreaks, otherwise
I shall be encased in drift,

Closed in the drying-ovens of the dunes
That blow and chafe in winds at night
Like innumerable church-organs, my meat

Baked into paper, the black thorn bones
Ripping through, all scraps blown away,
The skeleton so light it blows

Along the wind into the sea
Like a black feather, like the tumbling weeds.
I feel the heavy shadows lean

Upon the doors and enter, and put
Their blind gritty cheeks to mine, and I estimate
The crushing pressures and how, calling,

The fine grains dryly overflow the cry — but
The relaxation of the dead, light thing; ah
That is a prize, nearly transparent to the sun

Bone and skin like a torn-off insect-wing.

THE LAUNDROMAT AS PRAYER-WHEEL

I

The whirling pole bound up in linen,
The Lord of the Dancing Axle-tree;
There is a resurrection with a loud synoptic cry.

We move from place to place like shadows of the whiteness
Of these garments which seem woven of light
As they draw out of the mechanical sepulchre.

It is the night of the Mystery of White Shapes,
The angel is here, a splendid presence, like electricity in linen,
I fold the double sheet up, I wrestle with its wings.

The dazzling garments like dead bodies light the tombs
Of resurrection-devices, washing-machines in lines,
There are dancers full of water in the drums

That dance their twisty music to the coins,
Elastic celebrants treading in the tombs
Unwinding reels of flickering ghost-films.

The tumbling shirts are scalded fresh,
The hankies fluttering
Like the leaves of a white oak in a blowy cave.

The ghosts that appear in sheets!
Whisk the sheets aside, and what is under? Puffed water,
Geist, *Gischt*, gust or swimming foam.

When the neutron bomb explodes, it is the garments that
     survive.
A spotless white shirt falls shuddering to the floor,
A muslin gown settles peacefully to the grass.

He is clad in a cloud of fresh clothing warm and dry.
A really white shirt feels white when your eyes are shut.
The coffin-maker of Nazareth was a snow-white carpenter.

59

II

The superiority and glamour of a candid white garment.
As though wrapped in light, like a white-washed house,
I study the radiance of my shirt with my eyes shut,

As though wrapped in lightning, among the thunderstorms.
Men clothe themselves in dark in imitation of the clouds,
They darken their white clothing to show obedience

To the natural courses, the tinctured farmer bends
Over his muddy fields as the rain-clouds do.
Toiling in mud will not reproduce the lustre

Of low clouds as will acacia or indigo.
The naked body is vile, and lacking in speech,
The clothed flesh belongs to a man of eloquence

Whose skin of alertness converses with the hugs,
The featherings of movement, whose skin
Instructs him that a garment is a reservoir

Soaked in strength, and fabric a tunic of kisses
Like the heavenly tube through which the earth flies,
Arraying to their seasons, echoing.

Even the rain is white, and has a white belly,
Is affable, and clasps the gowned body
With its soaking grip in lighthouses of lustre.

LECTURE OVERHEARD

A great white ear floating in the sky, listening. I say
That your hair is but the beauty of ashes of blood
Passed out through your skin. I tell you how

We all live in our manacles which are
The food-chains forged by the sea. Light
Pours on to the brine, and the little creatures

Which are green dust thrive there, to be eaten
By the larger: small creates the great.
We munch the daft-eyed herring of that union,

We lift the salty waves of its flesh off the hairy bones.
The great tree of water flourishes over the sea
And begins walking on its visible roots

And then rain storms over all the land.
Holes are blown in houses, and their roof-scales
Lifted off the hairy timbers. It lightens and

Dissolved nitrates leach into the soil, the great
Thunder-voice utters fertility. In its echoes
Rings of trees spread out and protect our land

From the leaky repeated visits of the white water-engines
Of dazzling rain cranked out of the depths.
Grass spreads its tablecloths, and the cattle feast,

Our feast feasts. We pocket ourselves
Under open stone books and gravestones
But our substances distil in needlework

Of water back to the sea and there become
Dust-creatures and the shock-eyed salmon.
I have carved a large spider in wood

I have incised its globular body with the food-chains
Which wreathe about its jaws. See, the spider is hinged
At the edge of its carapace — open it — there is

A little carving of a baby, smoothly-grained,
Nestling deep in its spider-box, the future
Nested in the spider. The great white ear

61

Passes on, having overheard. We listen to the sea
Which renews, you can hear the reversal
Coming and going, with its sighs. The great ships

Pass by in chains, loaded with provisions.

FLESH THAT IS GRASS AND GRAIN THAT IS SPIRIT

He never listened to the sermons; a big man
He drowsed in his grey suits in the grey church
Like a statue folded in cobweb. A busy
Left-winger, he says church
Is the only time he has to snooze,
And if you ask him whether he's religious
Or only goes for show, he'll change the subject, thus:
'Equality reforms might very well start
At the centre of religious life;
Religious churches are the place for propaganda
Except they'd be more feudal even, that way.
To start with, there should be women priests,
But there, you see, you'd never shift them:
What, a bleeding priest smelling of birth-blood!
That would be too deep a religion by far; besides
Where would I snooze then?' But he cannot rest today,
He has turned the sermon off as best he can
But still the parson-drone bores through.
He turns it into a soothing hum — still
It breaches him with images: he sees
Painted on his eyelids a stone bowl, and beside it
A lighted candle, and he cranes his sleeping neck
To see into the bowl: it is full of barley —
And he must know, he gets up and shouts:
'*What was that*? say that again, Vicar, it was important;
You said something that made it all quite plain
Though I confess I was snoozing. Say it again.
It was something about stone barrels carved from church
    stones

62

For fermenting bright transparent barley wine;
What did you say then that made me see
Boulders grinding into earth, the barley-bed,
And earth turning into grain and grain to spirit
That inspires? Those living stones! That is factual,
That is something the common man already knows,
Something in those scriptures that is scientific
And religious too we ought to see done right here
In Church; but what was it you *said*, what text?'
A sidesman caught his arm, smiling with teeth
As white as lies, he smashed them, the people all
Turned towards him and then turned away; what he shouted
Was omitted from the papers and the Vicar would not
    comment;
The grey-suited snoozer lost his Parliamentary seat;

And since they hated awakening in their dreams, he retired
    to write
The Bible Designed for Sleep-Reading for those who did not,
Who would snooze with the mind open, and turn vicarious
    preaching
Into actual candle, seed, stone, ferment for dreaming.

ECCENTRICITY

I

A local yellow marmalade made with pollen.
Our neighbour steeps brass sheets upstream
Charging the river with electricity,
Holds himself responsible for the town's prosperity,
Runs for mayor. The farmer's boy hurries in
Shaking and white, having seen on the Green
Two newly-dead souls of cricketers practising
As stiff and white as if they had just been starched.
Bearing a child here makes you honorary Cornish,
But to whom do you apply for eccentricity?

63

II

For example, here is a man who wears a wine-coloured
Body-suit of tough leather fitted with
White nails and teeth and swagging paunch
The warmth and texture of Pigs. Is not such
A man death? Who could ever credit this
Middle-age! If you ripped
This false suit off would not life step out of it?

III

One applies for eccentricity to the Brewery.
I have seen many tribal, ceremonious masks, the best
A mask with moving parts: the face of a bird;
Twist a nail: the snout of a snake;
Open two more wood doors and we face
The mask of a man-bull, who is cattle
And rippling serpent, and bird
Wet from the egg all at once, blowing his flutes
With bull-breath, bird-beak, snake eyes.

I have a mask composed of earthenware, or glass,
A great snout of a pig of a pint of foaming beer.
Take that away, and what have you?
Perhaps nothing at all, except the same again, please.

GUNS AND WELLS

I

The artillery-men wait upon the big gun,
They have its banquet piled
And ready in greased pyramids,
They serve the long fat shells like cannelloni,
The gun munches with an explosion.

Molten tears silver our countenances,
Vomit of metal plates the cornfields,
Men blow away like smoke in the ringing brisants.

No doing of mine, says chef-commandant,
I feed the guns only when they are hungry.

II

She tells me the polished skull of a traitor
Lurks in this well still,
His comrades gave rough justice,
Over the parapet laid his bare neck,
Cutlass-sliced that smuggling head,
Which dropped like a boulder
And is down there to this day, she said,

Polished nearly to nothing,
Bobbing in the well-spring,
Folding and unfolding in the polishing water,
Almost glass, and papery-thin,
Ascending, descending on variable cool water,
Nodding upon a current which is a spine,
Spinning like a film of faintest shadow
Or flexile churchwindow,
Reflating when rain fattens the spring;

Then a sunbeam
Strikes down the brick shaft
And there gazes upwards, revolving in the depths,
A golden face; then the sun

Goes in and the water goes on polishing.

PLUMBERS AND POSTMASTERS

The noble plumbers, the entitled electricians
Of America, the very decent men
In tan shirts and sharp-creased pants as neatly pressed
And tailored as consultants' swallow-tails;
Their bags full of musical spanners, of steel dogs
That will worry the bolts, tease out the fused contacts;
Their hardhats and boots with steel caps,
And, marching behind, workmen's compensation acts;

Whose hands of leather brush the curls of kids,
Whose leather faces crease into wiring-diagrams;

Once the correct tool is taken from the partitioned box,
Time stops, and turns to a map and sequence
Of folds that fan and smoothe
Over the military shoulders of the broad shirt, turning
His fingers in your cellar, deeper than you guess.

Another Keaton face, offered letters,
Slides in and out of his chicken-wire hatch,
Bobs over his balances and scales of postage,
The brightly-lit sorting-tables behind him
Where all the sunburnt white-nailed hands
Pigeon-hole stiff white letters and brownhide packets;

On the muscled fingers
His fat diamond ring in which fortunate light is sorted.

MATTHEW WITH THE MAN'S FACE

The silverfly plucked free from the honey, safely.
The night is tangy with the mower, the cut stems,
Flies feed on the wheat's bled honey.

In bed the harvesters scythe still.
Does sleep want me? The mist develops
Four skeletal cobwebs in the clear hedge,

Brushed white by the misty cloud, parachutal.
I pick up a shell; I see the door askew of the new moon.
The trees give off glad odours, and the spiders

With white dew on their webs, dew on their claws,
Flash in the lightning, in fast talons
Gripping their meat that streams with dew.

It knocks me a mile back into bed, the thunder,
Bed that rustles like a white-leafed oak in a cave;
Bright quick filings of cloud knock at the window.

My skin is a mixture of lights,
The joint of meat is a symphony,
A lighted symphony to the flies,

My black transistor's choristers are dead silence,
The bowl of sugar is a cup of lighted bulbs,
Over our daily table we spread a black table-cloth.

The raw meat is a sexual pang,
They pack their sallow generations
In files of greasy eggs,

The back legs part and the packets,
The bales of netted eggs slide,
To them I glow only softly,

But the carcass in the moment of death
Sends out to them a dark beacon of passion,
For nutriment and practice, travelling grave.

In the quiet sun of summer
I sit in a fly's harness head
Soldierly with accoutrements,

Over me a green brass shine,
Cobbled with crystal lenses,
And during my life-time

The drowsy purr of my wings like a city
As the sugar-lumps light up
Like a distant city or the bowl of a lighthouse,

Matthew with the man's face holding the chrism biscuit,
The baby's body all slime and light, uncanny,
Flies like dragons of leather trampling the bible's leather.

THE WHITE, NIGHT-FLYING MOTHS CALLED 'SOULS'

I

Their bodies all uncanny slime and light,
I brush silvery maggots off my white bible.

We are copies of each other. Bound in leather
The book crawls among us with a loud voice,

Dead men's matter wormed into chapters
Between the first communion doeskins.

Worms are the messengers rustling in the print with quills,
Masters of God's word, the bible bookworms;

We are dead men's matter, gene-edited,
Say God's bibles, covered with worms.

II

The moths flutter at the candles like clothed ladies,
Like long ladies in Assyrian gauzes;

The moonbeams twine through the flowers creating nectars,
The moths sip, and reclothe the moonbeams in light leathers

And dusty gauzes like Assyrians for their dances,
And these moonbeam moths sup at the candles

Like soft explosions.
The sunshine falls on meat, creating liquors

The blackflies sip
Dressing bright sun in greasy leathers,

Tight shining leathers, and like Assyrian dragons
Trample on my bible-hide and kneel roaring

At top pitch, dabbing with their suctions.
The little bony flies come to the Bible

Because it reeks of sacrifice. O God,
Burnt offerings like blue candles of the ghats

Twirl in smokes of fat to Your motionless courts,
And we brushed the stout Baal-zebub flies away

That wished to wing Your meat, and clothe it, God,
In white maggot-skin, like bibles. The Lord's talon

Out of thunder slashes meat, scorches off the skin
Like opening His book, and He snuffs the odour,

Clothing the meat-nectar in the Lord God; and Who
Brings His own untouched flesh to His pregnant Bride?

III

The wireless at midnight gives out its hum
Like a black fly of electricity, folded in wings.

A moth like a tiny lady dances to the set,
This hum is light to her, a boxed warm candle,

This set has inner gardens full of light.
Our baby, like a moth, flutters at its mother,

Who mutters to her baby, uttering milk
That dresses itself in white baby, who smiles

With milky creases up at the breast creating
Milky creases, and milk-hued water

Hangs in the sky, waiting for its clothes,
Like a great white ear floats over us, listening

To the mothy mother-mutter, or like a sky-beard smiles
And slips into its thunderous vestry and descends

In streaming sleeves of electrical arms
To run in gutters where it sucks and sings.

PUMPKIN-EATER

I

His lodge is serpentine,
His awareness is the gold veins twined in the rock,
The green veins twirled in the tendril,
His belt is studded with stars,
He wears an emerald from which he chooses
The colour of his mother's eyes,
His lodge is permanent.

II

Yet she self-conceived!
She had the correct thoughts
And grew her pumpkin within herself,
His mother who wandered through the pumpkin-flowers
In rows, with scarecrows flapping like dark angels.

70

They were to her the potent flowers
With gold-sleeved knobs basking in powders,
They were the lilied voices of God
That taught her to say 'Here, I am Mother,'
And the light of it was in her.
She would wear yellow, as she expanded, like sails,
And, sailing past the pumpkins, she
Would smell like this, even in labour,
Especially in labour, and inhaled
The scent until she saw herself
Kneeling, with scarecrow wings,
In the patio where her double sat.
Proximity did it, proximity
And correct thoughts, and the smell
Of powders warmed by sun through gold petals,
Nevertheless he chose his berth and sailed it,
Travelled light as a perfume through the pumpkin-flowers,
Sailed the green-eyed lady in her blowing gowns.

III

The sun sinks on a column of firefoil.
All day it has been playing at protecting the pumpkins,
Denting itself in the foil pie-dishes
Nailed up to cross-poles under dusty sombreros,
Hung like glaring faces between the rows for scarecrows.
These capacious faces
Deep as the sun's distances
Flash and beam in the wind's knocks,
The sun-faced scarecrows should have the crows in stitches
Rolling with laughter between the green furrows —
They have always worshipped him,
And fed fattest under his august auspices.

With correct thoughts I feed myself a motherly pumpkin
Under the scarecrow dressed in my old yellow nightgown.
I will have the god in foal, I swallow his pips.
The pumpkin-plant winds round and round its green crucifix,
Flowers perfumed fists out of its lacy nightgown cuffs.

THE MEDIUM WILL NOT BROADCAST

His back is muscled like a pond of carp,
The muscle-fish glide and pluck
At the shiny skin, sweat-mirror.

He is in trance;
The numina show through here and there,
As in his back, as in the other side of the mirror.

The tambourine shakes, hissing, across the carpet-pile.
He says there is a rupture of the level paths
Of the ordinary world to let the spirits glide

Like loopholes that blow in long grass; he claims
'Radiant boys' attend him, like fire through grass,
And push loopholes into everything. They open paths

Among the beating scaly portraits which line
The river-beds, those oozy slowly-gliding
Galleries and corridors, where the fish hang

Beating against the current; sometimes these boys
Allow our draughty currents to suspend them too,
And float like masks of aether goggling at us,

And nail themselves up to show the ever-current
Of our own mirror-halls, our glassy ceilings. Broadcasting
    House
Is a ghost-station, its interior pitchy-dark

As a radio-set's inside, everything there
Has been turned into invisible wavelengths,
There is the ghostly thunder of the news

With ministerial shapes scudding a fitful sky,
And a rupture of level paths everywhere, and
There is a change of programme for we have switched
    universes.

But while he does his trance-work the house is a beautiful
    bread,
Under its tough roof of crust; entirely one
Beautiful atmosphere of new-baked bread

White and fluffy, that when he stops
Quickly grows stale and must be eaten up;
I see the spirits at our table eating trance-bread

Full of zesty yeasts, loopholes and faint alcohols;
Broadcasting House continues to broadcast ghosts,
But we turn away from those into our chain and circle

Of spirit sitting next to person, spirit, person.

THE GOD OF RESTRAINT*   *Tape B 4' 44"*

The God who holds his penis, denoting restraint.
The blue robes in which the children were created, with caps
And capes of crimson lace, in which they were created.

The babe in the womb clad in its kingly robes,
Blue lace and red lace, interlaced.
My father allowed the womb to draw its curtains,

To put on its garments. As I was born,
I was able to shed my mother's skin.
My father put on

My mother's skin to create me.
Our rivers here give of a semen
Into the atmosphere, a zest.

The baby's spit is clear applejuice.
The old, old dog, the silversnout
Sniffs the new baby and retires satisfied.

In the delivery-room there is a tang
In the air, like a semen. Outside
Are the avenues of tow-path trees

Rowing the breath of scullers not yet born.
A wasp wheels into the wind, blackgold flesher,
Drawn by the scent of blood-flowers, flesher.

I smash it across the window-pane and splash
Its clear applewater, but one must guard one's own.
It was five o'clock when the waters broke.

The God who signifies restraint after creation,
Whittled out of elm, the terminal tree,
When the womb-wall is raw, holding his cock.

A SHIRTSLEEVE WEDDING

I

The looped cross, or Venus'
Looking-glass; it decorates
Her neck; the neck
Reflects, the bush
Deliberates; in her belly
Your image grows slowly
In Venus' Looking Glass;
Will look at you, look back,
And ponder on you,
The glass opening its door,
The iris deepening.

II

The black and crystal faces
In the flowing river;
When I am liverish or disappointed

I always go down by the river
And watch the water in which everything I have seen
In my drunken fit is slowly washed away,

And in which the skull
Creates itself moment by moment. After all,
There is the baby,

With her mouth full of dew, and there is this air,
Which is like a Father, supporting all things.
The palms of my hands thirst

For the soft milch-mother who utters milk
Who uttered baby and who speaks tit-truth,
And for the deep

Skin of the baby but I may not intrude.
I walk therefore out of doors
To the river in the night,

The spark-holder of the elementaries, the starry
Tortoise. As the child cries from the lighted windows
A meteor falls in a cry of joy, this time. We had

A tieless wedding, a shirt-sleeve nuptials, the groom
And the bride wore loose shirts, and the she-baby
Wore within the bride's skin her folding and unfolding linens

Floating as veils float, as the shirt-tails float,
And she with her finger
Hushing her nose, peeking through the round inside.

III

At the wedding I thought I saw one of our oldest
Friends who is dead now, return in the mirrors,
As the priest pronounced, just for a peer, like a cloud,

A peek, as through a puddle in the rocks
Where the lacy hawthorn-blossom taps; I noticed
Him look because his shade was whiter than our clothes.

He was in mourning, in white of the spirit-land,
For when one is born these ghosts declare a funeral.
At puberty, shall the young people

Wear our clothes, shall they dress
In the shirts in which we created them?
There shall be their wedding too, behind the rock

Under the white-sleeved hawthorn which taps on it
And flows from its gnarled source
As the river does, and the baby in its mother-lace,

Leaning and tapping on its stretched drum at us.

SONG*   *Tape B 6' 44"*

I chuck my Bible in the parlour fire.
The snake that lives behind the bars there
Sucks at the black book and sweats light;

As they burn together, the codex
Flips its pages over as if reading itself aloud
Memorising its own contents as it ascends curtseying

Like crowds of grey skirts in the chimney-lift,
In particles of soot like liberated print.
The vacant text glows white on pages that are black.

The stars, those illustrious watchers
Arranged in their picture-codes
With their clear heartbeats and their eager reading stares

Watch the guest ascend. Around us in the parlour
The inn-sign creaks like rowlocks.
The drinkers glower as my book burns,

Their brows look black
Like open books that turning thoughts consume.
Then all at once

With a gesture identical and simultaneous
Of reaching through the coat right into the heart
They all bring out their breast-pocket bibles

Like leather coals and pile them in the fire
And as they burn the men begin to sing
With voices sharp and warm as hearth-flames.

The black pads turn their gilded edges and
The winged stories of the angels rise
And all that remains is our gathering's will

Which assembles into song. Each man sings
Something that he has overheard, or learnt,
Some sing in tongues I do not understand,

But one man does not sing. I notice him
As my song takes me with the others. He is
Setting down the words in rapid shorthand

In a small fat pocketbook with gilded edges.

PICTURES IN THE VINE

The ivy-tree snakes the house with scales,
There are near-gods hidden in the scales,
Administering, weighing, puffing, measuring.

Twigs clamber their ladders
Behind the heart-shaped leaves, waxy
And glittering like a waterfall

Plunging from the gutters; ivy creates
Dark-green corridors and travels them
With fibrous legs. And I, I am eating

Bread and honey on the chipped kitchen window-sill,
Sitting on the lip of the ivy-vine
Contemplating sweetness rounding in its spoon,

Surrounded by toad-creeping recesses dotted by
Nearly invisible dry webs. I sit
In the window of the plant the bees refuse,

Spooning my honey. Suddenly the mist
Enters the pages of the vine and develops
All its chasms. Every recess turns

To a picture of deeply-folded alps
Of tiny gathered peaks strung
With banks of snowy drops. The must

Of the vine, its compulsion-scent,
Reaches out like an echo of prayers
In a green vault, or like something yodelled low

On the watery peaks. The mist glides on.
I bite another mouthful, reach out past the vine
And touch a sunbeam. It is 93m miles high

A golden pillar, a swift-drawing flue
Smoky with food, as the bees know;
I taste the manna, and stay in place

Digesting bread and honey, until beyond the leaves
The stars emerge, illustrious watchers in their alps
With eager stares and clear heartbeats.

Is heaven not weakened by the weight
Of spectators in its hidden vine,
Will it not, before it cracks,

Send down more fibrous roots and plenteous observers?

ISLAND OF WOMEN

He had fallen into the same flesh as before.
All the mistakes were the same,
He was still to his shame only a man.

There was the silk-mill were he had worked,
Totally black and fire-satined inside,
There was the loom where he sat and burned.

Here is the bible he can read only when the sun is on it.
He loves almonds, for their taste and shape,
He says they are descended from Aaron's serpent-rod,

For their mandorla, their resurrection-shape,
Like a candle-flame of brown wood,
The oval door the Easter Jesus walks through, in his almond
    flesh.

Such wonder and astonishment could change everything, he
    said,
And in his astonishment he experienced
The god of emptiness and utmost life,

The god of widened eyes and held breath.
So this was his study, stuck with the same flesh,
And the greatest wonder, to him, was the island of women

So poor they darned with fishbones saved from the stew.
He wore their women's clothes, by their permission,
Sat with them in the evening, by the driftwood fire,

Adjusting his clothes around him, as the women did,
Settling the folds of a skirt, baring a creamy throat,
Adjusting the currents of that same flesh, he told us

That had so wearied him until it burned
In the flash fire in the silk mill,
The agony under the curtseying smoke,

And then waking in the same flesh as before
Shiny with grafting but no radical change,
Waking by an endurable fire, in women's clothes,

Among the women, by the greenflaring driftwood.
In the boat he wore, as everyone did, men's gear,
Among the shirtsleeves of the women, rolled to their work.

PHEROMONES*   *Tape B 8' 58"*
(Pheromones are 'external chemical messengers' given off by the body.
They are said to communicate profound emotional and physiological
effects from person to person.)

Dreaming of a dog, whose nostrils
Are his lightless eyes, means
Murder and riches; under the sunshine

Blazers bright as bluebells
With brass buttons yellow as butter;
The strong light

Shooting down the polished walking-sticks,
Running in sticks and streams,
Calls like trumpets

To the game;
The sea hedgehogged in gold,
Frogged in it, like a great blue blazer:

The great doorman with the labouring heart.
In this heat your scent is a snapshot,
Your spoor streams from you like a fragrant picture.

Your fingers
Sniff down your glass and walk into my lap.
It is so hot

My sex is a shelled snail,
And I excuse myself from You
For my nostrils wish to savour

The self-scent of my own sex
This gathering promotes,
And so my smelling fingers tremble first

At the eternal curry-smell of the brass handle
Of the metal of trumpets of the Gents
That it never loses or ever could lose;

Doubtless a dog would know its master
For over the brass in thinnest films are laid
The identities of all who have here touched themselves.

I bend my nose to the knob, for I swear
The champion of tennis employs this place;
I would know his sweat anywhere

After that magical game:
He filled the court with the odours of his perfect game,
Excellent musk, wiping his handle;

Let the trumpets call his prize!
I enter and am girded with personalities,
Long ghost snailing from the bowls

And gutters; my own genius mingles with that
Of the champion and the forty-seven assorted
Boozers I can distinguish here in silent music,

In odorous tapestries. In this Gents
We are creating a mingled
Essence of Gent whose powers

To the attuned nose
Are magnificent indeed
And shall affect the umpires

Who shall agree with what their noses
Tell them strides viewless from the urinal
Where the gentlemen sacrifice into stone bowls

In silent trance. Oh how
The tennis champion strikes pheromones
Under my guard with his far-sighted nose;

He has brought us to heat which calls him
In blond hair and buttons to his trumpeting prize.

LAMB AND LEATHER

The shorn white shadow of the lamb.
The lardy woolskin fat with blood.
The shepherds from the neighbouring tribes

Speak with sealed lips by covering
And uncovering their tattoos.
Great cliffs shaggy with salt confront us

Speaking with their tattoos of waves,
Great cliffs that shine like coal
And whistle like steam-engines

And hoist expanding plumes of spray.
Parson on Sunday, disturbed by tales of rape
Tells us that when Jesus leads the herd

Of Arctic deer, He is a gigantic stag,
Solid black lightning on His brow
Like the sun's black after-image in our veins.

This herd blazes like a flame
Consuming tundra in its path
With its constant shape and ever-changing flesh,

The great Sire racing at its head.
It is so large a god-herd
There is ample time for that Leader

To impregnate the mothers running
Who fall back foal-heavy into the stampede
And warp them there, the empty female

Dropping away and dwindling
Into large bones on the reed and sphagnum
While the sucklings race ahead

Before the pack has passed
To catch up with their Father, to challenge Him
Or receive His favours, running. He falls

Dwindling through the torrent of the hooves,
Like His emptied wives leaves behind big bones
And tines. The sound

Of this herd is like thunder
A new Sire sprinting at its head,
His followers trampling the bones of sires.

The human mother of the tundra
Wakes to this thunder,
And the men who shoot into the one shape

For meat and leather. She leaves her bed
To tremble at the flesh stripping its white road
Like a thundercloud grazing the earth

Thick set as rain with eyes of divinity;
You cannot palter with immortal flesh,
Shouts Parson, in the human race,

Or pause for private rape, but must
Take the mother of the tundra
While she still shivers to that thunder.

JABEZ IN COCKAIGNE

Once I had tasted the family food
I became a member of the family.
I, the dog, saw as they did,

More or less. Wind
Slid like a zip along the hedge, printed
Open louvres on the scarecrow's clear pond,

Sealed them shut again. I
Joined myself to my shadow
By masturbation. I took

The name of the dark Egyptian shimmering
Beetle known as the Sunshiner.
My lechery abated

And my vocabulary improved:
The snitch or snout
Became the knot of the face

Into which my chief perceptions
Conflowed, and I saw the urine-blooms
That I laid at each tree's foot

As signs of the spirit-traffic:
They strode along, roaring,
In bright slippers of my smell

And that of others like me, which made
Me humble. I learnt that whereas bones
Are the magnets of all dogs,

A lodestone is the pointing bone of God,
And that the daylight pours
From the open mouth of a star;

And I, the dog, have learned to ride
Horses, who have the heads of intent birds
And the strong ribbed bodies of boats

Between my four knees squeezed.
My dear family who created
Persons from the beasts and added to their own ranks

By feeding us with human flesh
So eventually we spoke, through clotted teeth,
Are hung with ornaments that tell the story

Of the evolution of all-living from the clashing
Rocks ground by blowing spirits, and the trees
Measuring their fruits out of that ground;

Make a harmonious clicking as they move
Which is the pebbly sound of that tale told.
Aware, with new nose, I paced my perfumed round.

I got married of course,
To a dog-bride in her wonderful odorous dress:
It was like the watery realm

Full of louvres and erasures;
She pissed my ochre dreams at me, this mistress.

DISCIPLINARIAN

I

The spirit of empty boxes helps you
Carry the full trunks.
Wet and shifting process, the sluice opens,

Hundreds of tons of water growling at the gates,
The reservoir pinstriped all over
With currents. He said that through

These miraculous glasses I would see
My aura as if my skin were planted
Thickly all over with waving grasses.

I saw nothing, but his intent suggestion
Opened my nerves and I experienced skin-rippling
Like a lawn streaming in the wind.

I thought it would be like a werewolf
Changing, then slinking with his hide
Brushing against long meadows, like

The whole striped reservoir trembling, intermingling;
But I was invisibly bearded, like the Lord God.

II

Then he showed me the shell; it was, he said,
The true shape of the magus winding through time,
Simultaneously present as an adult and coiling round

The protoconch or baby-button. I saw
Markings like a stretched face
Spreading over the nacreous, like a bearded face

That was healing slowly in the stone,
As though the face itself were fracture, blemish.
He explained that this was a nautilus shell,

But it was also like the man's skull who had
Arranged his days so that progressively
Larger domains of his life enwrapped the earlier with annexes

Like a spiral staircase rippling from side to side
With always increased chambers leading back
To the creative point, the beginning-exit. It was in this

Pattern that the magus sailed the sea of time
Raising his luminous tentacles like sails.
The beautiful picture excited me,

I felt my whole life skimming along on waves
Lit by the half-moon shining like a shell,
I felt I could see my life's patterns:

'Has anybody really done this?' I cried,
He said nothing, but shook his head
And looked wise. But I did it in my dreams

Where I inhabited great spinning homes
With windows of the sea foaming to the ceilings.

DREAM-KIT

Shut away here in Cornwall
With these provocative black
Materialising cabinets: TV or radio set,

That raise horrors and slight
Glories in the mind with
Invisible rhythms caught in

Their lightless black interiors
On skeletal fingers. The whole
Earth's atmosphere is a pond

Of trembling waves made
Of invisible colours, a river
Of transmissions full of

Coloured images of where it's been,
Its receptive water peering into cities
Full of troubling troubled ripples

The news makes and the dramatists
And the rainbowing commercials, and packed
With invisible creatures that swim

Plainly into view on the
Aquarium of your screen.
The set itself is like the window

On to a great tank of sharks,
Or one set into a swimming-pool,
Or into a river's banks,

You switch from place to place,
You have so many windows; it is like
A diving-bell searching over ooze

Or a tumbler pushed into a stream for you to see
The sportive minnows footballing
Back and forth over the green watery colours:

But they are all phantasms: you are watching
Vibrations only, rhythms, which are
Nothing shaking the radio-ether, which is

Nothing also. Racks and racks
Of goodly-looking nothing in a broadcasting hypermarket
Transmitting centuries of miles away,

And not at that moment either
Since these are only phantasms of reflections
Stored on tape, strips of plastic

Lined with finely-powdered forms of rust.
And these rays penetrate our brains,
Like God's rays of outer space

That warm us, but unlike those
Asking only that we remain
Distracted. The TV set

Is an artificial dreaming-kit.
The true instrument
Is the dreaming mind

That pushes its tumbler
Into the river that flows
Under the skin: the groping

Caressing fingers enter
The neck's skin and grasp words there
That cry out.

THE JOURNEY

Carriages sealed, and marked 'reserved'.
In the dining-car everyone turns
Frowning at something that slips out of sight

Past the window among the thundery horizons.
The clouds are like black cliffs streaked
With torrents of lightning, with the rain

Flying against the panes like an explosion in a glassworks.
Clouds like great white moths, wet moths
With the voice of an old lady out of control,

Mist riding over the gravel-pits like white Christians,
Mist on the steely waters like the cliffs of heaven.
I see stream past the window

A magpie like a black bible partly open, fluttering
Its white pages between black covers; it arranges them
So that some text is always showing; the wind

Flicks its pages and the bible spins past, and everyone
Turns to look again. One bible? What bad luck . . .
But here comes another, slowly rowing after the first,

Catching it up at last. Bible and counter-bible,
Man bible and wife bible: good luck for eternity.
The thunder has a human voice, now it is coming close

To having a human face: the clouds fold
Into a benign countenance, turning away. Behind its skull,
A bright shaft of sunlight breaks through.

On the rubbish-dumps I see the breeze still blowing
And the many feathery plant-seeds like travelling candle-
    flames.
They are burning rubbish-heaps like vast

Lantern-faces set in the hill, like a
Village of windows. I think that a city should not
Be hemmed by its disjecta, however beautiful

At night, but that it should be surrounded
By a wall carved to sound a fanfare on the dawn wind.
I observe this to the young lady opposite; she does not reply;

Her toes wriggle guiltily in their open-work shoes
Like a little stream over its rubbishy pebbles.

SOLOMON

The trick. The squint. The squint
Of the Ladyship, who seems to see through me;
The irises of the Green Man, focused

90

On the bridge of my nose, he appears
To have a mariner's far-sighted gaze, out of the porthole
Of foliage to the mythical horizon. It is a trick

Solomon used;
I mean my accountant, who is middle-aged;
He taught it to me. He would not discuss

Money, ever. He also loved this exercise
In Yoga called *Lion-Face*, where the mouth
Opens in a soundless roar, the eyes

Bolt and cross, the fingers go rigid
In talons; it is frightening: the mane
Of the man seems to stiffen

And ruffle, and like a field of wheat
Suggest images in its straw mirror
Of the breeze. He said, not accountancy, but

'That is my lord, the lion,' and
'All true men pass at death
Into the lion-form.' Whether he used

Such techniques in business, or for
Taming the Tax-Inspector, is doubtful; the vitality
That poured from these secret faces was frightful, and
        doubtless

Useful to him, and to me therefore. The images
I saw in his mane at these displays had nothing
Fiscal about them, they would trouble

My writing-for-money, my TV plays, with
Some unpleasant suggestion in the bland
Sit-com: a dead tramp in the doorway,

Stuck to his newspapers; a child
Plucking a ladybird's limbs like petals
Of a red-and-black flower that would not die;

91

In this Solomon seemed my opponent
Working against my larger profits. Outside
The office-window as the mane ruffled

And the soundless roar beat on the double-glazing,
The trees seemed lung-breathing headless giants all chest;
I thought I saw a bird flying with a tree's eye carried

Staring in its beak; and in the flowing
Tidal estuary the marks on the water,
The scratches and the gravures and the foam-flowers

Implied the passing overhead of a wing-system
Complicated and invisible as an angel
The mirror of the water could not send back to sight,

But which troubled its touch; the wind
Blows down the thermal corridor of the great sun
And is its wings and feathers of that which gives

Us light and heat of its own body, always. I thought,
As my accountant did Lion-face, of dying brains
Shedding their electricities like leaves falling; then

Of all the nights I spent dreaming
In my egg-shell position; then
Of my mother coming into my bedroom in her party-dress,

She had put fireflies in her hair;
And I thought how such thoughts
Would not increase my income if they were poetry,

And if not, why did they come from that ruffling mane
Of Solomon the accountant who scorned machines,
His index-finger telling my long columns, and somewhere

Lion padding deep within him like the engine of his soul.

SPIRITUALISTS*

Mimic insect-hormones
Secreted on their surfaces by plants
Have for millennial ages

Controlled these troops,
Our rose-tree was
Deciduous with aphids

Pumping out its juice
Into their dot-eyed flasks
And fluttering down white moults

In piles of leggy husks
Drifting about the roots.
The full skins toppled

From their drinking,
Plunged past the green stages
Crooked with living alembics,

Spilling back into the roots
Of the roses that are yellow
As very powerful ecclesiastical

Brass-writing, fiery letters,
Mottoes and commandments
Burnished in the furnaces.

The proprietors of the garden-stores
Very decent people subdued to their trade
Of plants and their gardening requisites,

Smelling of twine and useful tars, why,
He is a Spiritualist:
The roses are full of spirits

Sitting in their hearts of flowers
Which give forth their messages;
He hears them in church and there

I cannot smell his shop upon him,
The paraffin and the liquid fertiliser
That clothes his shop-clothes.

At the centre of this poppy
There are its stamens, ornamentally arranged
Round the fluted columnar pistil

Like a fountain black as soot;
It smells of musky chocolate:
I love chocolate and the flower

Makes my juices flower
As I watch the birds peck for nests
From the scarecrow strands of woollen

Fertiliser-smelling mittens,
And in the apple-orchard the trees
Are feathery as fowl with their white moss.

At night the apple-pickers
With squeezed eyes
Still pluck the fruit of their pillows;

Restlessly in their sleep
The seamed harvesters scythe still
As the emanations of wheat dictate;

And the spiritualist inhales
His bedside narcissus
Whose ancient oils

Command him to religion and trade,
Everlastingly flowing from their centre,
Perfuming breath and bones both.

ERROR

She said, lecturing, Mrs Golightly,
'All that was built by day was carried off
By the doves at night, past the tree of boundary,

The great elm, coffin-wood,
The tree of the terminus . . .' and I wondered
Who she was, Mrs Golightly, who told us

The very snow is shaped spirit in which every white particle
Has sat on the rusty decks of the milling blood,
Lecturing Mrs Golightly,

Whose bosom-shaped breath laboured endlessly
With bizarrest notions,
Of 'The Cow whose spirit is selfless

And dazzling, unreeling from udders
Like endless white cotton', Mrs Taffeta Golightly
Named after the rustling silk of libraries

Where consenting pages turn ceaselessly.
She had turned into a book that was talking endlessly
Read out aloud in rustling taffeta.

I would read her contents in silence, by candleflame
That trembles brightly, coming and going,
Her flesh coming lightly with delicate touches,

Bound only in skin, with its taffeta changes.
But then she held out her hands to the warm applause
And looked straight in my eyes; it was I

Who had misread; her taffeta spirit
Endless and dazzling had the power to show,
Naturally, lightly, that her words would come true.

FINIS

She falls and blurts
Her red shadow across
The pavement and the dented car-roof;

From the open goblet
Of her skull, the cortex,
The grey master, the two

Fat eminences fall loose
On their strings, like
The game of cup-and-ball

They sit like molluscs
On the inhospitable enamel
Glinting with frost

Stuck by their freezing lymph,
Like dead snails, like wet
Grey kittens. Her double cry

As she fell and as her lungs struck
Was like the twofold axe-stroke
That splits the primrose-yellow timber:

Her warning cry
As she swept from the roof,
Her thunk of severance.

Her convolved reflections
And suicidal resolutions
Steam into the air redoubled

In the shining blood
Like two twin tortoises,
There is a smell

Of brine and shit,
The air begins to scrub
With its rain, I walk

Into the little park,
The trees give off
Their evening odours

Like great dogs
Made entirely of green tongues
Gratefully panting by the hearth.

Every raindrop that falls
From these great brains
Has been by twigs and branches

Filed to brightness
And collects all
Available rays; and every leaf

Falls, and rises again, as I daresay
She shall not, and in the morgue
Of frost her brain crystallises to a tougher brick.

WET SPORTSWOMEN

The hoarse breathing of the dream,
The hoarse breathing of the dead living,
The dread of the endless breathing,

The endless bucketing, the measuring-out,
The well of the future that will run dry.
The egg chirping in her hand.

The little sparrow often flew
When she left the house, over
Her head, forecasting rain, chirping.

He descends through the bed as through a drum of trance,
He descends through the taut drum of trance as through a
    lake,
And there is that hoarse breathing, companion of the descent

All night. She is concerned. 'But
Let me tell you the marvellous dream I had,'
He says, leaping out of the bed,

His pyjamas yellow, 'I heard
All the clothes breathing heavily in the wardrobe,
Then rain spattered its mirror and I saw approaching through
    it

'A procession of drenched sportswomen
From "It's a Knockout" all in their luminous
Nylon uniforms pulsing with light at every crease,

'Which gave me special pleasure, and as they passed
A drop flew on my hand. I realised that its size
Had been measured out by countless forces as

'Our breathing is, and I lifted it to my mouth and drank;
It had been gauged by spinning of the earth and the sun's
    mass
And the moonlike luminous sportswomen twirling their suits
    of light,

'This embryo-drop, and it was in balance
With the flight of all birds and the hurricane of their wings;
I lifted it to my mouth and drank:

'It was as sweet as honey to my understanding
This universe-measured drop from the beautiful draggled girls
Birth-wet like the sparrow plucking at its egg-vault.'

WOMAN BENDING IN A FIELD

The mistress of the field who wears
A wooden bucket on her head,
The queen of the wet dust,

Her mantle trailing
An erotic, ghostly atmosphere;
She wraps her body in a coat of dew and straw

That measures rain back into drops,
The little pipettes exactly gauging
Each drop of the deluge, pulsing away

As an organ measures notes in humming tubes.
The lock of the bright heavens opens and the lightning flares:
It is her vizier. Afterwards

Her sheen lies over the ground like a pearly cloth.
At harvest-time the date marries her
As the storehouse. We think of lightning

As another husband
Unshucking himself from the dark clouds,
Biting, and hissing nitrate as he strikes.

Water pours down, like life that has suddenly undressed,
The datehouse shines in the downpour,
And the slate tomb measuring out its dates

A shining masterpiece of calligraphy, like the water
Combing through its gutters, like the protein
Of the date-seeds in their mother-flesh:

These epitaphs are inside-out,
Genetic writing within these stones
That shine as I suck them.

And as the thunder rinses my ears and gives me
Back my proper size, I swallow
The sweet flesh measured back

Into dates by the tall palm, watch water measured
Into pulses by thatched eaves among fields
Of water-thistles whitening as the clouds burst

In rain still warm from the lightning-flash,
Not the icewater that pours sometimes
From those rolling snow-cliffs that patrol above, and she

Out in her water-feathered strawcoat planting fresh dates for
   us.

THE SECRET BREAKFAST

The secret that was her marvellous beauty;
Sometimes he saw it everywhere, when he least expected it,
Though at any moment the bad habits would wear thin

And it was there in items of his person, or in what
He had not thought to look at before. He might suddenly
Catch a glimpse of it among the birds,

Not the song merely, but the flicker
Of white excrement muted
Between the legs could give it;

Just that phrase, 'muting a white
Excrement', with its flicker, could
Do it. 'Why,' he said, 'my world

'Is broken up in patches, little
Windows. The domes of the acorns
With their polish as of some Islamic masterpiece

'Infinitely jointed: they will have it. But
The oak is not my lover, only my friend.
Snatches of a friend's speech open to the beyond,

'The touches of a lover's hand are guaranteed!
But I will keep my scepticism,' he shouted,
As he walked into the breakfast room

And the table set was a sudden playground
Of toys, arbitrary and laughable shapes
That demanded to be played with; the spoons

Like paunching fairground mirrors on handles;
The boiled eggs like sealed skulls, full of a runny thought;
The salt like a caged swarm of pure white flies

In a fluted aviary; the pepper
Like beige gnats each with its pungent sting;
The fried eggs shining like the sun and so defenceless,

Blood of greasy gold; the napkins folded
Each in its ring like the silver thorax of a snow-moth;
Marmalade like an aquarium of orange eels;

The butter shining like a sweating steed
In its small loosebox; all the forks
Tingling with their tunes; 'Hum,' he said,

Watching the zoo parading and his actual breakfast
Coming and going, like poetry
In between the factual lines; 'Good,'

She said, not bothering about his hesitation,
But knowing he was happy, and that, in his case,
Meant seeing things, while

The eggshell fluttered in her white hands.

TURN OFF THAT BOX

Mr Pentecost is M.C. and has ordered the television
    disconnected.
Beginning with the carnival there will be many new
    programmes.
On the stalls I finger a dog-mask in papier-mâché and seed-
    pearls

And fat-handed satin ghost-dolls stuffed with softest feathers;
I am eyed by a stubble-haired ruffian drinking rice-wine at a
    rush-table
Near the open-air gallery of natural pictures in heavy gilt
    frames:

Landscapes of the tall hearts of trees and the sliced midnights
    of stones.
I consult a policeman in uniform like any other, except that
    on his
Moulded silver buttons the Queen is riding naked, on a horse.

The electromagnetism of wounds closing and opening
Still pulses on the air, the green surgeons of the drama
Still swim towards their tables, bright knives in their hands

And needles bright as gunshots for repair of wounds
Sustained by cops and robbers of the latter half-hour,
But who shall see them? Not the stones

Liberated, in their golden frames.
The sunlight is popping off the little waves.
We have poured clarified butter over these women

So they will shine in the dance like the sun, and
There is white mud made with oil for the moon-dance.
There are masks for putting on like sleepy poppy-heads

Moulded at the heart like the blind dead, dreaming in red
   collars.
There are skeletons three times life-size that will street-dance
Like jagged lightning on the black sticks of handlers;

And here are the bride and groom, modest in their marriage,
The whole town jigging round them dressed
Each in his own dream-picture, dancing; the happy couple

Who smell of skin and roses, married in that dancing.

THE HOUSEKEEPER

The long esparto of the nether world,
The grass avenues that rip you to pieces
Whispering *Isis*, *Isis*,

Go there a second time
And they restore you whole;
It is worth risking all.

The left hand of God is clothed
In a whispering glove of rushes,
Or it is clothed in a bed that creaks

Like leather; I found a great spider
That held fast like straps of leather tacked
Behind my picture of the Vicar smiling.

In the high wind, in the churchyard, he and I
See that the spiders are having difficult landings,
They have become caught up in their parachutes

Now their flight is hampered by a light drizzle —
They cannot raise their soaked webs, their windrows,
Their skyhooks, their gossamer strands

That lift them into the unknown by their
Bottoms where the spinnerets are; these matters
Blaze at me because my buxom pillow

Waits for the kephalia of my teacher, while the yews
Distil their flashing poisons over the indifferent graves.
I will seduce him from the church

With the empty foxskin
That wraps my full white bosom; after
Through the mists and jet black graves we'll wander

With the light gone out of holy marriage,
Religion changing hands, and all the old
Arguments gone. The sea goes on

With its distant signing on all the beaches,
White writing on gold. I draw off his limbs
Jesus' black shroud of cleric's cloth.

My master of communion
Lies flat on the pillow like a snake flattened
On the superspeedhighway, crushed

And recrushed by the speeding traffic,
Its venom evaporating
Harmlessly. I have tried

The taste of the cloth mask of his chest,
I have loosened his linen collar with my teeth,
Rustling *Isis*, *Isis*, and he comes

Like an express-train, calling on
The thousand-windowed name of God; and now
It is the yews distilling slowly on the mirror-graves,

And the marriage gone up the chimney where the cats shriek
On slanting roofs in midnight moonlight. My cup runneth
    over
And my house is as if full of holy bread new-baked,

A tough flaky roof and inside
One entirely beautiful white bed that must be eaten
Smelling of love's light alcohols and yeasts

Before staleness hardens it like holy marriage.

RETURN FROM THE ISLANDS

I

When you die, you are a shadow,
A cool wind in a feathered garment.
This is the rock with the sheer sides where they hung sailors,

The gallows-rock that wears light like a shawl.
Rowing over the slaty water
That matches the clouds, two people

Seem suspended in the sky;
There is no horizon.
The rock is packed with horizons,

Millions of years old, in strata.
It is a tip that shows above the water,
And a very draughty rock,

And the feathered gulls visit, rising and falling
On shafts of air like elevators.
In the white flat of his cap and the blue of his jersey

He steers skilfully his boat
Away from the whitecaps raised by the fresh breeze
Over the jersey-blue waters of the morning.

The rock where they hung sailors is now
A jagged trapdoor in the bright broken sea-floor
Where the waves like white-capped sailors hang and fall.

II

The wet calculators shift and gleam
Behind his concentrated stare,
He is writing out a sum in a long pink book.

He tears the cheque off, hands it to the boatman
Who looks at it with an eye poached like the sky.
Signatures fall scrolled out of the open white skybook,

And wet our clothes and print our skins
With the distance they have travelled; we can read this sum
With the pink sight of our skin. His cheque-book

Is empty and he tucks it away; one needs, he muses,
Human life as a rest from bliss. The boatman
Takes the tiller and launches into the bright sea,

And into his guide-lecture on the dead volcano
Of sacrifice and its lava stiff
With shiny skulls like shells or seafoam.

There are clouds settled on the mountain
Like great white moths clasping it
In their wings; a little liquor falls

From their gentle scales. There is more mist on the water
That dazzles like the cliffs of heaven as they return
And as they pass slowly back to land like spirits

Rowing through the mid-sky who need no quay.

THE YACHT-PARTY

Better weather moved in
And swiftly disconnected the waves
From their shackles, their looping, ringing

Slowly-shifting chains.
The yacht moved on through a cell of calm water.
I admired the elaborate coiffure

That was drawn without a face, in black ink,
And which hung above the mantelpiece,
I was told it was a Leonardo, in pen and iron-gall ink;

Sometimes it was a coiffure, and sometimes a much-twisted
    trunk.
There were cocktails, and many marvels on that boat,
The black girl was wearing rubies and nothing else,

The white girl sapphires. We disembarked,
There was a mist over the flagstones.
It was not like

The lighted warm ports of the yacht-party:
The windows of the flesh were shut tight,
And we knew we would not believe in their closure

Until the moment when they opened up again,
In another stateroom, on another sea;
There was so much to remember, that would lose its tang

Abruptly; the marvels in ordinary,
Rich things. I remember their leisurely billiards
And the whitebeam cues that struck the spheres

Like an allegory of the planets, or of the wind
With its invisible cues rolling the leaves
In rustling bundles; I remembered

Mystical dialogues with the millionaire Egyptologist
Who told me that the gilding of the phallus
Meant the gliding of the phallus as the warm sunbeam

Glides into the skin, the mouth, the eyes.
He wanted me to go to Egypt, where the lighted ports
Of the skin are never bolted, and I agreed

But he would not be reminded in the morning, and we
    disembarked
Among the hail rattling like hobnails. He showed me
An ancient medallion of a spirit-child

Fed with apples by a wolf; on the reverse
What he told me was the hairy *Wateress*, her throne
Speeding over the flood; we were ourselves

Enclosed in our millionaire's throne and state
Which was full of detail and the bright light
That money sheds, one house of many mansions on the water

Speeding. Just for an hour or two after we left
The great yacht, we were people lit inside
Like houses in winter, sailing into the snow,

The shutters in the skin wide open to the cold.

SPIRITS

The milk is soft as soot,
Sweet and white as sugar.
The baby cries and is not cold,

She cries under the seagulls' mewling,
Under the skylight, in the bassinet,
She squirms, turning in her shawls

Round and round. I show her a picture of
Venus staring in her looking-glass,
She reaches mewling for the god;

I show her the beckoning old
Burning one, the almond-eyed
Cyclops of the candle-flame, and she cries

Because I will not let her suck at it
And she reaches for its warmth.
A white gipsy blows from a fissure in the lawn

And dances like a candle that is all
White flame: it is the local name
For eruptions from the ground after downpours,

And the baby stretches out for this cool phantasm
In swaddling too, the dew breaking
From her little mouth, and running down

Over the bare shining gums. She frets
And nibbles at a biting-toy; the tooth
Is rising as a star rises. Thus the spirit

Grows in hard whiteness from
The soft white milk that feeds it like
An endless cotton unreeling from the mother,

Sewing the garment that the ghost wears.
As the mother holds
The full-fed milky child, it is to her

Like holding sleep itself full of dreams
Of spirits manifesting, and so it is to me
As I drowse by her side like the child,

Feeling sleep roll off her and into me
My head swimming in dreams, my man-paps dry.

SHORT SERPENTINE AT THE LIZARD

A various and most questionable animal
Not caught easily except with the left hand.
Earthworms sculpting images of themselves

Out of bowels, coiled seamanlike, in fresh earth,
While the rain splashes on the window, hatching snakes
On dribbling glass that scent out mulch,

The great soaked tobacco of the grassheaps.
The fresh earth is speaking aloud to me.
The earthworm has the globe in one embrace,

The river Kaka, the swallowing earth-mouth
(And the Kak drops from God ascending the seasons,
His wormcast, bright banks of flowers to us).

So worm eases through the jetstream, it is
Both latitude and longitude,
It is the sea-serpent, and at that size

It sings triple-bass and flashes with lightning,
Coils seamanlike the high silver clouds;
That lightning is the telegraphese chained in its nerves.

It swims Amazons copious as itself without fins,
By undulant expertise; you may tread on the worm-cast
But you cannot outrun the serpent, not

On your horse. It unpicks the fingers in the graveyards,
We are compressed into it as night slides on,
Into darkness under its belly, the crooked one,

Called crooked, but as smooth as wheels.
The carver sells me a memento lighthouse at the Lizard;
'What is it carved of?' 'Why, Serpentine.'

THUNDER IN EXETER

A weir of leaves from the felled tree
Throws out its water;
It is best to lie down in thunder;

110

The oaks dancing in wet bast masks
Pause for excess of blue-white light,
Stand still in the flash

Which is sugar and bacon to them, they lap it up.
There is a tang in the air like a felled cry
A mark in the air, a mask in the air,

The great bolt darts into the well
Like an express-train galloping
Lighted windows through a tunnel;

The shaft echoes
Like an organ with a great cry,
Billows with steam, ozone and brilliance,

And current runs like blue mice
Through Exeter's riddled cellars
Along the small pipes wailing and hammering.

Goldfish sip at the new water from thunder,
They glow under the sooty cloud
Like coins struck by lightning,

The shell of the well
Moans still, and the snail-backed cloud
Shrinks back into notes of rain

Light splashing in innumerable small thunder-packets.

PLEA

To enter the motionless courts
Of the Lord God in a fair
Religious shirt, not too frilled,

Not too much throat;
To be called to judgment
As a fly, a mummified Pegasus,

With a helmet of iron;
Or as a bear, and to protest aloud
One is a man, and to spend

Anguished time
Soaping and shaving
One's hide of hair,

Hoping to conform and
To become quite passable, except
For the claws and muzzle, while

The soapy hair falls
Slowly through the cloudy marble floors
As does all matter extraneous to heaven

Descending meteorically to earth
Or as the aurora which is cremation
Of briefs and pleaders, but so far away

It is like a folding of light; one knows
One is pleading well by
The firm feel of the paving underfoot,

If it grows mushy
One had better start again
With improved counsel.

They gave the bear
Wings after all,
Great wings with bear-brown feathers,

And soon his bristles grew again
And he was all bear,
Angel-bear. Should I not withdraw

Into the forests to learn growling
At strangers in honour of the Creatrix
In the North, never hoping

To survive these courts
With false whiskers and paper nails?

VENOM

I

A cat rips its metal with another cat,
Then it tears its calico,
Then it weeps like a hurt baby.

It is, as they say, on the tiles,
And you can hear the toms drumming the terrace,
The whole length of it.

Though my house is sometimes as it were
Made of bread, new-baked, holy,
A tough roof of crust

And inside one entirely beautiful white bed
That smells of love's light alcohols and yeasts,
That bed hardens as the years pass,

And when the cats screech the same cries,
When they rip their screaming tin,
Now I listen to the meaning scrupulously

Of some of those destroyed cries.

II

I saw the moccasin snake flattened
On the superspeedhighway, crushed
And recrushed by the speeding traffic.

It looked like the spread tyretrack of a skid
Marked with the herringprint of bones
And its venom had evaporated with its snake-blood,

Harmlessly. It would all wear away soon,
Or the cleaner pick its hem off the road,
Strip it off the asphalt with his spade-edge,

Hold it up to see the snake's X-ray
Against the petrol-light,
Like a bearded savant in a clean museum,

Reflecting on a specimen among glass cases
Full of the headlight of unused venom,
Breathing venom, listening to venom

On the superspeedhighway like a lashing snake.

GLITTER

The backward child, caught in some dream,
Sitting at the sheer edge of the day, of the dry
Shadowy paddling pool in the children's park,

Hunched shoulders, large face white
As her china-white shirt, placid,
Vacant and shiny as a little puddle

That does not hold the reflection of the cloud
That sheds it: the flip side
Of a Zen master. The other children

114

Brawl and tumble in the dry pool, illustrating
Each other's dreams, the river nearby
Polishes and polishes, it polishes the sun

Thin and gold, and polishes quarters from the moon, and all
The old iron thrown into it, which bleeds
A long time along the river in roping strands

From feathery bedsteads down to the sea
Like throbbing arteries. It polishes that
Red-haired suicide down to his bones,

It rubs the print from old theatre programmes,
Unpicks them to a cloud of gnatty fibres. It rules
Its own furrow, polishing its roots and stones

Until they are buoyant grains, no more
Than a glitter in the water, like stars; it polishes
Old bottles until they lose their stiffness

And bow on the currents, until they are
Almost water themselves. A thought
Floats behind the child's eyes, and she reaches

Under her skirt to polish
Her furrow, until the thought is glitter.

THE GOLDEN POLICEMAN

She is today a combination of angel and doll.
Somehow she opens certain doors in the air.
The shell is warm and scented by the sun,

Rests in its light-fracturing sandbath among
The enormous shuffling nostrils of the dunes.
My skull is a creating gate, like the shell,

Echoing without question the sea's shuffling
Which is an excellence like touch.
There are little sandy spiders with their eyes

Gleaming like shoebuttons. There are
Granite boulders on our beaches,
And powder-puffs on her dressing-table.

The dew falls and crawls like the ghosts of spiders,
The waves come in like long cripples or snakes.
A policeman wonders about my reverie, which has

No visible means of support, until he looks round
And sees her too, salutes, and resumes his beat
Like the waves, policing.

His clothes are made of the shadowy look of misdoings,
His hickory truncheon of fines, his notebook
Of broken commandments. I stand by the dock of hulls

With this lady, and the sun breaks out of the clouds
Dusting him with gold, by some means
She has transformed the Law;

And I am very content, listening to the steel hulls
That ring like a run of bells to their riveters,
Like cathedrals made entirely of bell-metal,

Though the notes are low, very low, and listened to
By the soles of my feet more than my ears,
And beside the dock with its beached shells

The wind furrows roads through the sandy rushes.
The Law puts back its notebook, buttoning up his breast
With a golden stud stamped with her image, or

One like it; he has spoken a few words
Into his portable radio, which occupies his
Heartside, and he pauses to watch the water

Far out on the estuary patrolling
In its blue uniform. He looks like a projectile;
His helmet could be lined with stars

Like pricked velvet. As he tucks his notes away
New doors open and rush towards us across the ocean.

DECISION

We hold our assembly
Under the mothy galleries of trees.

Firing his stubble
This defendant sowed

Five fat fields of smoke.
In the dry summer his blaze

Like a blowflame
Threatened the sheltering valley

Through the windy corridor of the hills.
Our meadows would have burned down to the beaches,

The red-hot rubble of the shores.
We made him defend himself

But his plea was overwhelmed
By the soughing of the argumentative

Poplars, the clouds
Of leafy witnesses. He looked

At us pleadingly, then
The clouds burst, and the crowds

Of water hurried past babbling,
All shouting and glittering

Our prisoner was reduced
To a shining shadow, our judicial robes

Drenched on our backs, heavy to earth
Like sopping leaf-heads,

Their hems weighted to the ground
Like tree-roots; we raised

Our faces to let our silent
Mouths drink up the water

As the trees did; we all knew
The facts the weather recapitulated,

That a lucky thunderstorm
Put out this criminal's fire,

And he did not create
The dry summer either;

And this was our sole action,
That as the rain fell

On the court under the open sky,
We were mindful of how we are rooted,

And he, the guilty
The only one among us

Who caught cold,
And in his fever

He will burn like the valley grasses,
In his sweat drench like thunder.

Autumn is beginning, the grass-stems'
Dry riggings trapeze their husks,

The domes of as yet uncandled cities
Gleam in their scaly cups,

The acorns plummet
Their unfelled docks for wooden ships not hewn.

SILENCE FICTION*   *Tape B 14' 54"*

The late houses are built over the early caves,
The foundations and cellarage are where the first people
    lived.

We have fitted stout doors and hang their keys
High in the chimney-vaults where, out of sight,

They gather from the flames great swatches of soot,
Bunches of soot-flowers out of the food-fires,

Like the brushes of black foxes through the generations.
Then in the especial bad times a besmutched woman

Enters in defiled white to fetch down our keys
And open the earth to us. As she stands in the threshold

We know we must cast over our hearth pitchers of water,
And she treads through the warm ashes and with black
    sleeves

Reaches into the hanging soot,
Unhooks and rubs across her skirt revealing

The bright metal under the black grease. She
Throws the key down ringing on to the stone flags,

119

Leaves into the dusk for the next house.
We unlock and descend into the cellar-roots,

Light in the chimney-roots our lower fires,
And begin our lives on the unadorned earth floor

Some of which is sheer sand, elsewhere silky clay.
There we find shells of earliest cookery, and our fingertips

In the dirt encounter marvels of red-ochre bones,
Our torches tossing shadow like black potter's clay.

The wind blows through the upper houses, and the rain
    blows,
Cleansing hearth and porch, rinsing chimney. We know

By no messenger when to return; under the tangled
And matted hair, and the grime, and through the rags

That have rotted, a look shines,
An acceptance. Then we return

To the sunlit chimneys and the whitened hearths,
Out of the earth cradle; quenching the flares,

Troop chattering out of the cellar stairs,
Draw baths and strop to mirror-glass the rusty razors,

Secure the lower doors with their immense keys we hang
Shining bright in the chimneys; light our upper fires.

The black soot feathers through generations on the long keys.
We recall wondering, occasionally, that in those cellars

We never spoke, not at any time; once through the door
We were to keep and breathe the silence

That had gathered there like foundation water
In the roots of the chattering houses, deep and pure.

MAD SPEECH CONCERNING DRESS

God's husks are rustling in this cottage press.
Flinging shirts over the bed sends Him sprawling everywhere,
His white moults, the pure shadow His so-brightness casts.
His holy cloud passes on, but its simulacra linger,
Their rows of buttons like sparks of Him.
This drawer-handle is a long museum
Since I have feelings in my fingertips that see
Personalities printed on it endlessly,
Showcase of all that take the shirts to wear;
And the soiled clothes intolerably record
Every tug and action through the day,
The fibres sip up traces of the meals, and harsh
Syllables soak out as I cram them in the wash
Quick as I can before I re-live that day.
So my thoughts are snagged in clothes
I turn and overturn, in the laundered shirts soft smells,
Soft pure smells like nuns who have walked
Through misty gardens of clean soap, and cloth
Sewn and buttoned in His image, woven like veils
That clasp to Him, which He's always peeling off
In multitudes that fill the shops where people don Him
And go about their tasks creasing with reflections,
Expressions, the many masks of God
Littering the adulterous bedspread, wrinkled, ripped.

I creep in God's husks, ecdyses. The wind rattles them.
I know that people slip off their white corpses
When they are dead, that cannot be cleaned
Or ironed or slipped on again, so it is said,
And they wear clean linen like an outer soul
Lined with corruption. What, I ask,
Of the inner soul, underneath the dung
That lines the folding masks, that speak their dirt?
That is invisible, and God is too,
Except for these husks that are rinsed with sunny air
And purged by hot irons. I know I am dazzled
By the God of the White Shirts, but how can I love

Anything but His forms, which are husks?
Where is He, or the soul? I look down myself
And see I am clothed in His expression in great folds,
And I feel through every crease of Him, and throw up my
 arms

Like white wings. And I haunt the crevices
Of this cottage full of His reflections, and is this house
Also a shadow of him, when he hill-stood, and the cliff
Another empty face of Him, and does he shed
Or print the cities upon the ground with his tread?
Folk drape themselves in Him and stand enrolled
Small-faced above the great-faced folds
In His radiance and with His frowns that strike across
With great commandments as they toss
Their bodies in His draperies which are changing
Tapestries of scripture with a different law
Written and erased each second, and sometimes I attack
And rip away this veil of mesh,
This page rewriting itself to start afresh,
And this is how they found me, naked, tearing my flesh.
And then they tied me in wet sheets like frowning faces.
Now I am the falsifying laundryman since
The whole earth is dirty, or am I the servant-boy
Of God's erasing angel washing the grimy records,
The steaming shadow-faces, since when I pull them out
Of the soapy water and hang them up they grin
All round me in the sunny air, and when
I take them down it is to serenify and pleat
Them back into the way they should be, perfect shirts
For the mad people well enough to walk the wrinkled streets?
The laundryman should be spotless in a clean room,

And I pray that He will teach me calm
Working in God's presence when He environs me with balm
Of soaps and clean shirting which are crucifixion-drapes
Over our skins; calm in His presence of those shops
That buy and sell Him in neat boxes packed
With new fresh faces to clothe our backs with,

And all the warm cupboards airing like harness of white
    wings
The spotless linens, like flesh on hangers
Awaiting animation. I am death-angel
Making immaculate by process, yet Your trueface
Winks and suffers somehow in those folds,
Your manifold countenance in the soft cloth tosses
In turbulence and agony buttoned to the weave of crosses
That underlies all I handle, and which washing dazzles.

All the light blouses drift by like summer ghosts.
Can I ever pass a blouse either
Without shuddering and showing? My skin
Needs all skins, his and hers,
All at once, woven in one stuff, the many faces
Folding into one Countenance. How shall I learn
To spin my skeleton out into a splendid white shirt,
To unravel veins and all tubes of me into a weave,
A magnificent damask shirt fit for a babe's skin:
I am becoming one who desires to clothe
A Second Coming, and on the line the shirts
Buttoned up, trumpet with their tails
The only issue for my need. How can I clothe all?
It was done for us, once, the Clothing
Of the Five Thousand from a few rags, that bookcase

In the lower room full of tomes
Like leather boots all shining tells it that way, yet as I read
The fingered pages in my clean clothes, I flinch
And wish clean new-paged books opening like snowy bread.
I draw the heavy curtains and light the lamp and read
While God's frowning glowers from the drapes, yet I believe
One day the drawer will fly open of itself to welcome Him
Who will form His radiant skull from all the grime about Him
And a shirt will unfold from cellophane like crackling
    blossom
And the winged leather books of theology will shoe Him
For our journey, and He will wait not moving, so I can see
Him motionless and smiling with his single mouth and offering
His foamy white-sleeved arm to me like my brilliant son.

WET ANGEL
College Green, Bristol
(*For A.T.*)

I Dried Angels

The fountain felt out with its spray,
In the hot city at a touch of breeze,
My skin wanted to drink it.
The white pass soaked me and made me naked,
My skin was water, my shirt rucked with it.
The fountain sprays a chancel with living windows
Over its stone altars shining wet;
Opposite, the cathedral sits as in dry dock,
Barnacled with gargoyles.
I am sure that the water comes from the church,
Condenses in its damp crypts,
Runs like a reverse fountain
Down the walls and between the chinks of flagstones;
I think it sucks water from its congregations:
They say 'Aaaaaah' and they say 'Meeeehn'
And they say 'God forgive us' and mean it,
And their breath smokes in the chill grey air
And is caught in drops on bearded gargoyles,
And on the barbed corbels,
And in the creases of the stone foliage
Like the sweat of a petrified tree at dewtime,
And runs down into the crypt like water of prayers,
Staining the old saints' bones and eroding the skins
Pressed flat in heavy vestments studded with stones,
Softening the leathery hearts of God that are flat as pages,
Sinking deep into dead wells stuffed with hair,
Then somewhere under the written stones turns round,
Pumps back again into this open air
Like a dazzling white shift of a flower
That feels me out with its spray,
Which springs on glass stems in the summer Sunday.
It wants me naked among its petals
Drinking with my skin the prayers and responses,

124

Taking them back into a living body,
The dry Christian people who have expended themselves,
The skeletons on dry benches in the dark cathedral
That smells of beeswax, incense and the bones,
Packed into pews like cords of wood,
Hollow as insect-shells perched in a dry dark tree,
Cicadas emptied of their song. Now the fountain
Springs in the square like visible song,
Look! and in the breeze that wetted me,
That saunters on beyond the ironbound portals,
The God-people inside float a little in their seats
Like leaves that need water, and rustle, like dried angels.

II A Transparent Mollusc

A glass octopus in the square, balancing arms.
Where is the head then? Deep below the earth.
The arms spring out of the fountain's centre
Like a cup with a spring in it,
They have wriggled through the city like merchants' fingers
(Purified of cash and only busy, ghostly)
This water is their soul separated from their goods

And their water-souls are let out to run like city-children,
Look! their spray etches the water-surfaces,
I see faces cram the mirrors,
And as the gust that wetted me passes,

The fountain shudders and steadies;
For a moment all the souls of the city
Looked at me from the water with one head.

The fountain juggles with its body,
It is never the same body twice,
Will water ever fall faster than water provides?

And the drops wet me so I am covered
With smiles and faces,
And wet kisses which soak me through my clothes.

125

III Passing the Ghost

The fountain's rigid path.
An iron motor hammers in an oily box.
Water sledge-hammered through stiff pipes.
Water shocked into ghosts through an iron tit

In a concrete basin, like a wine of light,
Electric-powered: its ghost-heart
In the generating-stations
Is a fountain of current a county away,
Ghost driving ghost through the wires like cool pipes,
(Touch that blue spirit and it jolts your ghost out
Like a sere water that sucks your juices dry):
Water stands on it, mowing its white arms —

And behind this blue ghost a black one stands
Black with millennia of sunlight which it gives up
Mowing and yelling in the power-house fires,
And the generators pump, passing the ghost along,
Casting a bobbing shadow of water, which is white
As God's shadow, which is like the clouds
Cast off the mirroring sea by the sun's fountain.

My fingers pass through the balancing water
Like so much clear shadow. When the spray comes
Grazed from the water by the wind's passing
Like the syllable of a ghost too large to see,
The water bleaches, is white as a nude
Who stands and spins, and a nude

Drenches like sanity.

IV Memorabilia of the Mystic Spout

A water-flower, pumping in a square.
He watches his own breath, returned to him.

The citizens stroll past, breathing clouds
That roll upwards off the city streets,

126

Then fall on us, or coil across the maps
To fall elsewhere, and pump in city-squares.

This water-prick glistens from adventures!
It has entered many bodies, pulses with its tales.

How dare he watch it, kingly lingham!
With the white skin creaming as the street-wind grips it,

And fertility patters on his shirt
Like a gusty message from another world,

Like a coiling tongue that flared and spat
From a glassy lung of water. It is his own shade

Whitening in the mirror,
And Bristol's ghost too, and his own

Day-to-day bodies, all of them, and the bodies too
Of his fellow-citizens, in one white bride.

V

A gust spatters his shirt. He jumps.
The spray blows, and wheels round, and catches a girl
In flowery silk. She jumps, and glances across the prickling
    bowl
At the wet stroller who shares her wet.
Her inner water flows and his fountain twitches.
The sky-fountains gather from their corners.
The whole city is about to love a wetting
Or not, as the case may be; between the man and woman
The fountain plays with its saturated robes
Where the air billows, in sleeves like silk.

VI

The city-water touches them softly,
Dabbing his shirt, her skirt,
Water saluting water. All flows.

She is not the same water she was yesterday.
She cannot mourn it or conserve it:
It flows. This is why her father, maybe,
A Christian City Father, called her Rhea.

In winter it is raw glass full of cobwebs,
It is furred like slashed lace, it is full of cogs,
It is white as bride and maids glass-etched,
It is nuptials for a season. But Rhea flows.

VII Shooting a Jesus

They planted this water-tree in the stone basin,
This stream standing on its source,
It cools the square for contemplation,
It was not intended to empty the church
(Like a nightmare bus-station
Announcing nothing but departures) on sunny days
With undershapes of water
Turned into a sunshine show
As though the silver screen became the star
Leaning out of her light to touch my shirt
Over my heart leaving a wet bruise.
A schoolboy has a pocket full of stones,
He pulls his arm back and pumps the gravel through
The fountain's body
As if he wanted to stone a ghost
Or shoot a Jesus
Who resurrects an infinity of times,
Who has been through you,
And through the body of this girl here,
And through the crowds and through the city fathers, and
    dances
Clothed in wet skirts, emptying his church.

THE APPLE-BROADCAST*   *Tape B 18' 16"*
(Meditation-experience at Boscastle, N. Cornwall)
An Apple a day . . .

I

A valley full of doctor apples,
A valley-stream like flaming straw,
The valley blushing from its roots, and rustling,
The hill-roads cobbled with red fruit.

Some hidden bird blows his dry trumpet
Under the oaks, hoarse as an insect
Crying, under the crisp fretted oakleaves,

Hoarse as a fly walking in its hair,
Its swishing skeleton, its crackled footsteps,
Over the tusked leaves, hoarse as broken bone.

The air goes taut on water-strings
To dirigibles of thunder riding, it splits,
We see the lightning packed with apple-valleys,

All the insects shaking, and their shutters shine
In repeated flashes, under the lightning.
There is the dry trumpet from the rustling leaves

Of some bird chopping at the oak-line
Full of green caverns with the dew
Running over every twig forming

An eye wherever it can,
Waking up from the sleep of water,
Shaken into the sudden light,

Tall water-being shaped by fretted trees,
And the hoarse bird trampling over the leaf
Under the green caverns with its dry trumpet,

While I lie intensified among the grass-sheaves
By cobwebs in their flashing wheels,
An instrument among bird and insect instruments:

The oak-walker scrubbing with its throat,
Or the spider's wiry grasp
In its silk aerial hung, catching parched transmissions

That cry with dry coughs
Out of their saline drops
That moisten their batteries of wings,

The moisture that looks out of their dry eyes
Which the spider blots up with its tusks.
A bird speaks like crackling porcelain,

Like the crunching of its sky-blue shell,
The lightning flashes over the apples,
The black birds skid across the red roads,

And I lie as if transfixed by the lightnings
Amid the stiff dry arrow grass
Near the Spider with her crisp handclasp

In her glass ladder rocking the empty fly.
A dog barks a command from a cottage yard,
The apple-college shakes

Over the entire valley.
On the upper road a quarry-lorry
Hits a bump, its boulders bark and spark.

II

The valley full of doctoral apples,
Round doctoral books among the spider-webs,
Scarlet with white sugared pages;

The oak-colleges ponder in their timber halls
To the bird's music of the dry oak-trumpet,
The wasp demented in the apple-crags

Turning over and over the red book
Of tattered skin and fragrant learned oozing,
The bird barking under the trees from far off:

That standing wave called 'Bird with Dry Voice'
Held in branches, broadcast in echoes;
The broadcast 'Valley Water' flashing and rustling;

The birds sailing on their silky circuits
Among the laddered robes of water,
And transmissions whistling in these vivid outlines,

Their skirts that brush us constantly
Hanging from stars, their sparking silks,
The enormous white voices over the wet apples.

III

I listen to the voices in the rock cottage
I dwell in which is a radio-set,
I go outside and watch the planets brush us,

Their wakes of birds and insects, their broadcast
Called Spider in her silk antenna.
The stars shine down in their long dresses,

Every cell of the grey house becomes glass,
The skin clears of each red apple, every seed
Like slow lightning spreads in orchard-boughs,

The enormous white voice over the apple-valley
Beats in echoes orbed like spider-webs that shine
In broadcasts hung with appled water-drops,

131

Its electricity races down all streams and stems
Like flaming straw and mirror appleskins,
The stiff grass stands on end.

I am electrical for ever with these sights,
This broadcast uttered from the apple-storm,
Beneath my skin its lightning runs for always;

Like cobbled groves of rosy apples
I will transmit my programmes,
Like insect-eyes glittering under lightning.

IV

In the valley full of doctors,
In the weather full of round young doctors,
The lightning is a white priest hurrying
Past fat black convocations far above him,

And the red doctors knock heads conferring
Like the rolling green heads of the sea close by
With white beards and rumbling snowy rafters;

In my granite cottage which is a crystal-set,
The walls flashing with their ancient broadcasts
Recorded as the rock flowed, then set in wavelengths,

The baby sits with fingers weaving programmes,
Sitting in a broadcast which is a jersey,
Picking up a programme which is a rusk,

Mouth full of dew, fingers which are aerials,
Sitting on a wavelength which is a blanket
Woven out of meat and starlight on some far hill;

I will give my baby an apple which is a doctor daily,
We shall tune in together to what it says,
Breathing apple-scented air-transmissions,

For with my tender knobbed antenna
I tuned into a certain star babe-broadcast
Deep in a girl's receiver

As every bird and beetle and doctor apple
Does, on its own particular waveband.
There is so much unseen, and so many tuning

To lightning broken over the apple-orchards, responding
To lightning spun through white-skinned orchards.
Now the thunder has closed his humming station,

The moon-band rises, moths dressed like moonbeams
Take wing into the excited grasses.
The Spider plucks some for their floury blood,

Good bread, but many couple
Lamb-faced in their woolly wings,
Tumbling like moonlit monarchs in their ermines,
And printed across with black star-signallings

Flutter the constellations on their wide white wings.